8/22

MODEL SOLDIERS IN COLOUR

Model Soldiers in Colour

ROY DILLEY
and
PHILIP STEARNS

BLANDFORD PRESS
Poole · Dorset

First published in 1979
by Blandford Press Ltd,
Link House, West Street, Poole,
Dorset BH15 1LL

Copyright © Blandford Press 1979

ISBN 0 7137 0907 3

British Library Cataloguing in Publication Data

Dilley, Roy
  Model soldiers in colour. – (Blandford colour
  series).
  1. Military miniatures – Pictorial works
  I. Title II. Stearns, Philip Olcott
  745.59′282   NK8475.M5

Set, printed and bound in Great Britain by
Cox and Wyman Ltd,
London, Fakenham and Reading

Contents

Introduction

Among the many hobbies and pastimes with which we can enrich our leisure moments, one of the most rewarding in its exercise both of artistic and practical talents is that known by the generic term 'military miniatures'. This term embraces all aspects of modelling: the making of original figures, vehicles, scenery and so on; the construction and conversion of commercial designs; painting and displaying the models; and the collection and embellishment of 'toy' pieces. The subjects of the hobby are primarily of a military character, but, since military life is a part of life in general, a good deal of what might be called 'civilian' in context is inevitably represented.

So popular has the hobby become – especially over the last two decades – that there are many thousands of its practitioners throughout the world who are members of organized clubs and societies, and as many again who pursue their interest individually. The standards of work achieved by leading military miniaturists deserve the highest praise and consistently result in the production of pieces that are truly *objets d'art,* eminently suitable for their frequent public exhibition in museums, galleries, great houses, shows and conventions in many countries, as well as in the cabinets and showcases of private collectors.

Sculptors, designers and artists of outstanding ability and reputation are numbered among this hobby's practitioners, and the ranks of its professional designers contain those at the summit of their craft. Yet whatever their level of competence, the vast majority of enthusiasts derive enormous satisfaction from their efforts, are content to improve where they can and simply to enjoy the hobby to the full in its rich variety of subjects, skills and techniques. Perhaps the popularity that military modelling has achieved is due to some extent to the appeal that it makes to so many interests, presenting its historical, geographical, biological, artistic and technological aspects in an easily assimilable form that is pleasing to the eye and stimulating to the imagination. Few other diversions can offer so much colour, excitement, information and opportunity for the exercise of creative and artistic talent.

Just what *are* military miniatures? They can be defined quite simply as representations to scale of fighting men, their auxiliaries, supporters and contacts, with their dress, weapons, equipment and other paraphernalia, and the environments in which they exist and carry on their activities. A pretty broad scope, it may be suggested, but that is attractive in itself, since whatever a person's profession, character or special interest there will almost certainly be some aspect of military modelling to appeal to him. Almost every vocation, profession and trade is represented among the hobby's devotees, many of whom also take an active part in one or more of its associated activities – badge-collecting, researching of uniform data, prints, photographs and so on – which not only provide accurate information for the construction and finishing of models but are also valid and absorbing interests in their own right. It follows that the military miniaturist will acquire a great deal of background knowledge concerning his modelling subjects, their environments and their period, all of which is useful general knowledge as well as valuable in practising his hobby. A newcomer to its ranks who intends to take his interest seriously (not meaning, of course, joylessly) can look forward to projects that will test his inventive and practical abilities to the full, and at the same time afford enormous satisfaction and relaxation.

However, one should strive to avoid pomposity in talking of advantages and benefits; the plain facts are that in all its aspects the hobby results in much that is good to look at and to enjoy. It has been said that 'everyone loves a parade', and the saying holds good in this context, to judge by the reception commonly given to exhibitions of military miniatures by the public (who often turn up in their thousands). Not only parades, but also battles, campaigning, life in home and overseas garrisons and other facets of the military scene can be colourful and fascinating subjects for models and delight the observer. It is hoped that the examples illustrated in this book will provide knowledge to the uninitiated and confirmation to the addicted of the attractions of military miniatures of all kinds.

We have tried to cover as wide a range of subjects as possible, and to include examples from the work of outstanding contemporary modellers, both professional and amateur. Obviously, for reasons of space, much that it would have been agreeable to include has had to be omitted but, nonetheless, a sound impression of the hobby's scope and attraction can be gained from the photographs. No doubt in the interval between the compilation of the book and its publication many pieces of superlative quality will have been produced. If the reader of these pages finds an interest in military modelling awakened or revived, their purpose will have been accomplished and the authors will be content. As with all pastimes, indeed all occupations, experience has no substitute, and first-class results are seldom achieved overnight, so the tyro can be urged to persevere; the established to continue the search for new techniques; the expert to strive for even greater heights; and the casually interested to look again – there may be even more to military miniatures than at first meets the eye!

1

Historical Background

Although the creation, collection and conversion of model soldiers, guns, vehicles and equipment – known collectively as military miniatures – is now a pastime that is enjoyed world-wide, it is probably only since the end of World War II that such activities have acquired a solid, 'respectable' image as a genuine art-form. Public approval of the hobby is expressed by the many thousands of people who, though not themselves active participants, nevertheless throng to exhibitions and displays of modellers' works, there to admire the skills, imagination and ingenuity that go into the creation of military miniatures today, as well as to indulge their nostalgia for the playthings of youth. Yet not so very long ago, miniatures, models – call them what you will – were manufactured, purchased, enjoyed and regarded by all but very few 'eccentrics' as toys pure and simple, however excellent their design and craftsmanship (an attitude prevalent since the introduction of commercial pieces in the eighteenth century).

It is difficult to draw the line precisely between miniatures which were intended for decorative or votive purposes and those whose prime function was as playthings, but certainly military figures of one sort or another have a long history – examples carved in wood were recovered from the tomb of an Egyptian prince dating from some 2,500 years before the birth of Christ. Other ancient peoples also produced small representations of military subjects, many of which – made from all kinds of materials, from bronze to stone and wood – survive to this day, having originated in long effaced civilizations of Europe, the Mediterranean, Asia Minor and the Middle and Far East. There is evidence that lead soldiers were cast in moulds by the Romans, incorporating a considerable degree of animation and detail. They must have turned them out in some quantity, but their precise purpose is not clear. It has been suggested, however, that they could have been used as aids to the teaching of tactics on sand-tables – an early form of war-gaming indeed!

During the Mediaeval and Renaissance periods military models and figurines appeared from time to time, as toys or *objets d'art*, but in both roles they would have been costly, and ownership was probably limited to the noble and wealthy classes. Several illustrations in contemporary manuscripts depict 'tournaments' – games involving contests between miniature mounted knights and/or foot soldiers – and several specimens of these types of figures have survived as museum exhibits at, for example, the Bayerisches Museum in Munich and the Kunsthistorisches Museum in Vienna, and on at least one occasion in an exhibition at the Tower of London.

Sets of soldiers, forming complete armies with guns and other warlike engines, made their appearance in the seventeenth and eighteenth centuries. One such formed a collection assembled and kept in the Armoury at St James' Palace, London, for Henry, Prince of Wales (who died in 1612). Another, cast in silver, was given to the Dauphin, later Louis XIII, by his mother Marie de Medici. He cast figures of his own to add to the collection, which, when inherited by his son Louis XIV, was further expanded and supported by an ingenious mechanical contrivance, the brainchild of the celebrated architect and engineer Vauban. Unfortunately, the

12

precious nature of the metal from which this marvellous army was made proved to be its downfall: during a period of financial embarrassment the King caused it to be melted down to provide money for his Exchequer! Though made of gold, and so even more valuable, a later royal model army, that given to the infant King of Rome by his parent Napoleon in 1812, escaped this fate and still survives in the possession of a noble French family, the de Pierres, to whom it was presented by the Empress Eugenie, mother of their previous owner Louis the Prince Imperial.

Model armies were owned by other royal and noble families in Europe and Russia, but whether made in wood, metal, plaster, or more unusual materials such as edible gum, starch, wax or *papier-mâché*, few pieces from them have survived. Many, alas, were destroyed in various political upheavals; others were victims of the steady attrition caused by time and use. Comprehensive collections of hand-coloured figures printed on paper and cardboard are also known to have been in royal hands during these times, but they too have long disappeared, and their appearance and composition can only be conjectured.

The figures referred to so far – with the possible exception of the little Roman lead castings – were all, whatever their basic composition, the property of the extremely well-to-do, but towards the end of the eighteenth century techniques were developed that enabled durable model soldiers to be produced at prices that placed them within the reach of a much wider range of people. Initially made of tin or pewter and cast in engraved slate moulds, these pieces were of the 'flat', two-dimensional type known as *Zinnfiguren*, and were produced in the Nuremburg area of Germany by a number of master designers, the principal and 'pathfinder' being the brilliant Johann Gottfried Hilpert. 'Flats', the 'steadfast tin soldiers' of tradition immortalized in Hans Christian Andersen's tale, were economical to produce, reasonably easy to distribute by reason of their lack of weight and bulk, and resistant to damage under normal conditions of play, display and storage. In time an amazing number of subjects were covered by the flat ranges, not by any means

13

confined to purely military affairs. The individual pieces were often designed to a very high artistic standard, and recognized scales, adhered to by most manufacturers, meant that the products of more than one could fit comfortably together in a single collection, thereby encouraging sales. The production of *Zinnfiguren* flourished, and although the industry suffered a severe set-back with the destruction caused by World War II, it still survives soundly, particularly in Germany. Properly painted and displayed, *Zinnfiguren* are among the most elegant examples of military miniatures, particularly effective in mass presentations and cased dioramas.

At much the same period as the German masters were starting their work in Nuremburg, a Frenchman of genius named Lucotte began to produce fully modelled *figières* in Paris, also cast from tin, antimony and lead alloys but sold ready-painted. Lucotte's miniatures could be marketed cheaply enough to make them available to a fair section of the public, and the firm did extremely well, combining after sixty years or so with competitors to become Mignot, which operates its factory and sales organization in Paris, still producing figures and accessories of high quality after nearly two centuries of existence.

In the mid-nineteenth century, German companies – probably as a result of the success of fully modelled figures by French manufacturers – began to turn out three-dimensional or *ronde-bosse* pieces, perhaps the most famous of these being Heyde of Dresden. Between them the Continental firms had established military miniatures, flat and fully modelled, as viable commercial propositions, and the range and scope of the subjects they represented were amazingly wide and varied. Not surprisingly they dominated the market, exporting their products to an ever-increasing clientèle throughout the world and firmly entrenching the model figure among the familiar treasures of childhood by the closing decade of the nineteenth century.

At this time cast models in one or other of the lead alloys were all produced as solid items. *Zinnfiguren* were, of course, merely thin

14

sheets or leaves of metal, but *ronde-bosse* types used an appreciable amount of material in each casting, which added significantly to production costs. Seeing this as a trading weakness that could be exploited to his firm's advantage an English toy-maker – William Britain by name – with an established business and some knowledge of hollow-cast metal techniques, began in 1893 to market the first examples of hollow-cast fully modelled figures, each being, as it were, a thin shell of metal, which made it lighter and much more economical in its use of material than a similarly sized solid piece.

So successful was this new venture that William Britain, with the enthusiastic assistance of his large family – most of whom contributed their organizational and technical abilities to the business – rapidly built up a range of models. Commencing with British Army subjects, the firm produced more and more representations of foreign troops until, by the year 1900, there were over one hundred different sets of models available. Fresh designs, many based on well-known military paintings, continued to appear, found ready markets and showed steady improvements in standards of modelling and finish. Britain's soon overtook and outstripped their Continental rivals to become the world's largest manufacturers of model soldiers, a position which they have maintained right up to the present day. A number of other companies took up the manufacture of hollow-cast figures with varying success, but none achieved quite the range and quality of product that distinguished the out-put of Britain's Ltd. It must not be forgotten, however, that although the 'solids' no longer dominated the market, production was still continued, and by and large the undoubted high standards of quality were maintained.

The early years of the twentieth century, before the outbreak of World War I, can truthfully be called the hey-day of the metal toy-soldier. Abundant supplies of all types were available and prices were such as to bring them within reach of all but the very poor. It was possible for many an enthusiastic child to amass or 'collect' an army of models, with horse, foot, guns and transport all complete. The seed of what was later to develop into the great, ever-spreading tree that is the military modelling hobby of today, may well have been sown in those halcyon years leading up to 1914.

Most manufacturers turned to the making of munitions during World War I, but model soldiers were still produced, albeit in much reduced numbers, and the war was the source of new models – figures in service uniforms and with much of the heavy weaponry of modern warfare. The inter-war period saw the flow of military miniatures swell again into a tide, augmented by new series of farm and zoological models, and other subjects of a less martial character. In Germany at this time metal was in great demand for real-life armaments, and a new material was developed from which model soldiers could be moulded. This was Elastolin, a compound of glue and sawdust; it set hard and provided a good basis for the application of paint.

In 1935 the British Society of Collectors of Model Soldiers was founded, the first group of its kind to be established in the world, and one which would have in the future (under its revised title the British Model Soldier Society) a most profound effect upon the whole military modelling hobby. At that time, and for the next few years, the ranges of soldiers, weapons and equipment to be found in the manufacturers' catalogues were truly amazing, and it is doubtful whether such comprehensive coverage has been achieved since then, or ever will be again. It seems probable that all production of military models ceased soon after the outbreak of World War II – certainly it did so in Europe – and the factories of famous companies in the field were once more given over to the making of munitions. Miniatures were not to be manufactured in any quantity again until after 1945.

By the early 1950s model-soldier firms were back into full production in the United Kingdom, Europe and the United States, bolstered by a new phenomenon: the bespoke figure craft (it was by no means an industry yet), in which gifted artists turned out individual, unique pieces to the specific orders of collectors. Soon firms were established, of which the first and probably most influential was that of Norman Newton – later called Tradition –

16

whose output of high-quality solid metal figures was aimed directly at the increasing numbers of collecting enthusiasts. Societies, too, were proliferating, spreading still wider the growing interest in military miniatures, and the work of talented amateurs in creating their own figures or 'converting' the products of toy and connoisseur modelmakers was becoming ever more technically and artistically excellent. The interest in military miniatures was really under way now, given added impetus by the advent of a new class of materials – the plastics – whose suitability for the production of models was quickly realized, being cheap, tough and able to accept and retain a maximum sharpness of detail in the moulding. Plastic assembly kits, in which many parts were put together with adhesive to make a single super-detailed model, were produced in vast quantities, covering figure, vehicle and equipment subjects, often to a very high degree of accuracy, and, most significantly, at reasonable cost. By the middle 1960s production of hollow-cast metal figures had totally ceased at Britain's, and since then their toys, at least so far as figures are concerned, have been almost entirely moulded in one or other of the plastics, with a very restricted line of solid metal items in recent years. Towards the close of the 1970s we have a whole complex industry encompassing figure manufacturers of all kinds; specialist book, magazine and print publishers; adhesive, paint and accessory producers; and artists, writers and designers – all catering for the military miniature hobby, with devotees throughout the world numbered in tens, if not hundreds, of thousands. It is interesting to speculate what the situation will be at the end of the next decade.

2

The Golden Age of the Toy Soldier

In the preceding chapter it has been related how the mass manufacture of figures ('flats' including printed paper types, followed by solid and later hollow-cast *ronde-bosse* pieces) made them available to a much wider range of clientèle than before. These models were designed and marketed for use as toys, and although the occasional enthusiast amassed them as what would now be known as collector items, it was as playthings that the overwhelming majority were bought.

To what can their tremendous popularity be attributed? Certainly they were comparatively inexpensive; undoubtedly they were bright and colourful; substantially they represented the costume and actions of their real-life counterparts with reasonable fidelity. More significantly, however, they symbolized the military life with all its apparent glamour, splendour and excitement in an age when, under the spurs of nationalism, colonialism and imperialism, countries were evolving and frontiers were changing and expanding, requiring the services of professional soldiers without necessarily involving the bulk of their fellow countrymen. Children could follow the adventures of their heroes, reconstruct the campaigns that were being reported in word and illustration in the periodicals of the time, and indulge their patriotic fervour by means of the humble toy soldier, without ever seriously intending themselves to take up the profession of arms.

Whatever the contributory reasons may have been, what is sure is that toy soldiers in their millions captured the imaginations and enlivened the play-hours of generations of children during the latter half of the nineteenth and first half of the twentieth centuries. What brilliance and panache they presented to the world, these armies of miniature warriors; with what pride and enjoyment were they paraded and manoeuvred; and how much affection and nostalgia did they inspire when the passing years caused childhood's treasures to be laid aside.

As we have learned, it was the metal hollow-cast figure, principally of British manufacture, that dominated the market in late-Victorian and Edwardian times, the period in which it achieved its maximum popularity. Troops of nearly every European (and many another) nationality were represented in ceremonial and campaign uniforms together with their horses, guns, waggons and other equipment. Miniature forts and castles were provided for them to garrison and defend, frequently serving the further purpose of receptacles to store them in when not in use. The very boxes in which models were packed were often decorated and illustrated with information about the real-life regiments that their contents represented, and manufacturers in general showed a surprising insistence upon high standards of accuracy in the moulded and painted uniform and equipment details of their miniatures.

Quite frequently the work of one or other of the military artists of the day, especially that of Richard Simkin, provided the inspiration for a model's design. Painting of toy soldiers was normally an 'out-job' performed on piece-work rates by female workers in their own homes, trays of unpainted castings being delivered by the manufacturer, who called again after a certain time to collect the finished pieces. Of course to maintain uniformity, paints, brushes and 'patterns' were supplied to each worker, but it is quite extraordinary how closely these guides were followed, and how each manufacturer's distinctive style was maintained when it is remembered that scores – perhaps hundreds over the years – of individuals were contributing to their production runs.

The designs and finish of the Britain's products were, without doubt, the finest in the hollow-cast category. As might be expected with such a successful enterprise, Britain's did not lack imitators and competitors – many of whom, until prevented by copyright restrictions and injunctions, had no scruples about blatant piracy of designs. By and large, however, Britain's products were superior in qualities of figure proportion, casting and finish, though other reputable manufacturers turned out hollow-cast pieces of considerable merit and commercial appeal during this period. Among those whose figures are most worthy of mention by virtue of design, finish or other features, are John Hill and Company, trading as 'Johillco', James Renvoise, 'Reka', the trade-name of C. W. Baker, Hanks Brothers, C. D. Abel and A. Fry. All contributed something to the attraction of the glittering ranks which lined the shelves of toy departments in great stores as well as neighbourhood toyshops and played out their roles in parades and battles on the carpets and lawns of homes all over the world.

Hollow-cast figures were produced manually from hinged metal moulds attached to projecting handles frequently incorporating asbestos gloves to protect the operators' hands. Molten metal – an alloy of lead, tin and antimony – was poured into the mould, given a quick swirling shake to force it into the engraved detail, then returned to the crucible, leaving a thin shell around the inside of the mould cavity. This shell was removed on opening the mould and was revealed as a fully modelled figure.

A characteristic of hollow casting is the small round aperture or blow-hole left at the point where the surplus metal flowed back out of the mould. This was not usually obtrusive and indeed was frequently obliterated when the model was painted. Some later designs of hollow-cast figures had one or both arms movable; there would seem to be little actual advantage in this feature, but no doubt it had its purpose even if only as a sales 'gimmick'. One more way in which the hollow-cast figure scored over its rivals was that it was easy to repair if its head was broken off. A used matchstick forced up into the base of the head to form a spigot, then similarly pushed down through the neck until both metal parts were re-united was all that was necessary to restore the little soldier to 'life'. Sometimes a dab of glue would be applied to strengthen the join, but more often than not it was felt to be more advantageous to allow the head to be turned realistically on its wooden 'spine'!

It should be remembered, however, that, although heavily out-numbered, solid cast figures were still available in considerable quantities and variety, particularly on the Continent.

With so many and diverse pieces at his disposal, it is not surprising that the Victorian and Edwardian child often conducted battles, even campaigns, of considerable complexity, bringing into use sundry arms of the service, infantry, cavalry, artillery and the like, and occupying large areas of garden, nursery or playroom floors, even sitting-room carpets – sometimes to the detriment of his relationship with his parents! Winston Churchill recounted, in memoirs of his childhood, how his father had been moved to wrath by the enthusiasm with which the youthful Winston, striving for more accuracy, had introduced real stable muck into the quarters of his miniature chargers! How many other parents must have viewed with mixed emotions the effects of miniature field-engineering on prized lawns and cherished flower-borders, not to mention the scars of sundry spring-propelled missiles on floors, wainscots and furniture. Perhaps they consoled themselves with the reflection that at least these depredations kept their offspring relatively quiet!

To assist the budding General in his employment of miniature forces, Britain's issued in 1908 *The Great War Game for Young and Old*, a manual which included text supported by illustrations of both model and real soldiers in colour. During the next five years no less celebrated an author than H. G. Wells published his *Floor Games* and *Little Wars* volumes that were to enthral adults as well as children, and laid the foundations for the wargaming movement which was to spring up some forty years later. It is true that types of war-games, *Kriegspiel*, and sand-table manoeuvres had been in existence for many years, but it must surely have been *Little Wars* that caused them to be practised at all widely. Unlike the war-games of today, *Little Wars* involved the infliction of 'casualties' upon opposing sides by firing at them with a toy cannon. The projectiles were lengths of thick metal rod, moulded lead slugs or pieces of wood dowelling, and the targets needed to be struck over for a hit to be registered. Such treatment was hard on painted castings, and an enthusiastic practitioner of this type of game could often be distinguished by the somewhat battered condition of his forces.

Fortunately for many figures, and for the pockets of parents, a great deal of the use of model soldiers was in play of a less damaging and more imaginative nature. Favourite pieces were treated with care and jealously guarded against the attentions of their owners' more boisterous or destructive relatives and friends, and such warfare as was practised was observed more in the form than in the actual battery and mutilation of its leaden protagonists.

There were at this time, of course, adults who took a keen interest in model soldiers, war-games and so on, but their armies were still very much composed of toy pieces with little or no alteration or additional decoration. Commercial finishes were attractive, reasonably accurate and relatively durable, sufficiently so in all these respects to satisfy the requirements of all but the most exacting of customers. The play and miniature warfare that was carried on was uncomplicated – as the reality must have seemed to those not directly engaged in its prosecution. The Great War of 1914–18 changed that attitude drastically, with its uniforms that (whatever their nationality) became drabber and more business-like, its ever-more powerful weapons, and its rapidly developing technology. Inevitably, the model world reflected its full-scale counterpart; toy soldiers in drab service uniforms made their appearance with improved guns, motor-lorries, even some aero-planes, while only the most imperceptive children failed to realize

22

that warfare had become a far different matter from gallant, chivalrous combat between gaily caparisoned opponents.

After the war military figures were widely manufactured again in ceremonial uniforms, but the active-service types remained and were added to, and other lines were introduced: farm personnel; animals and implements; zoological specimens; figures from the hunting field, circus, and other civilian pursuits and activities. Probably as many, if not more, models were sold in this period, and certainly the manufacturers' catalogues were filled to overflowing with troops and equipment of all kinds as well as the new varieties of figures mentioned above. But now ceremonial was quite distinct from active service; Britain's catalogue actually listed their types under these separate headings. In the model world, as in real life, the Victorian/Edwardian 'summer' was over.

3

Flats or Zinnfiguren

It would be misleading to refer to *Zinnfiguren* only as model soldiers, for the genre is by no means confined to the representation of military matters. Soldiers may in fact form only a minority among the multitudes of flat pieces produced over the last two hundred years or so, and since in real life military service co-exists with civilian pursuits, mingling and reacting with them at all levels in peace and war, it is not unreasonable to include an account of 'flats' in a work mainly devoted to model soldiers and their ancillary equipments.

Although it is possible, even probable, that many pewterers and workers in other metals in France and Germany included some flat toy soldiers among the other multitudinous knick-knacks that they turned out, it is generally accepted that Johann Gottfried Hilpert, who was born at Coburg in 1732 and moved to Nuremberg in 1750, first established the manufacture of tin soldiers as an industry in its own right. Hilpert's brother, sons and nephew also carried on his work, and the initial successes of his venture quickly led other craftsmen to follow his example. Thus was founded the Nuremberg 'school' of makers of *Zinnfiguren*, in which the names of designers such as Ammon, Schweigger, Haffner and the Heinrich-ssens, father and son, were to feature largely over the following hundred and fifty years or so. Other groups of engravers of flats sprang up in Hannover, Berlin, Erfut, and Brunswick in Germany and included the redoubtable J. C. Allgeyer, who later included half-round pieces in his production. Although models were made in a variety of scales, the 'Nuremberg' size – 30mm for dismounted figures and 40mm for cavalry – became standardized, principally through the efforts and example of the Heinrichssens.

At first *Zinnfiguren* were indeed cast in pure tin, but the delicate nature of this metal and its high cost soon caused a substitute to be found, an alloy of tin and lead which was both stronger and cheaper. Small amounts of antimony or bismuth could also be added to the alloy to improve its 'running' characteristics and retention of fine detail, but the exact proportions of metal in any manufacturer's alloy was a matter of some professional secrecy. By and large, the requirement was for a metal that was reasonable in cost, tough (yet with some flexibility so that it would not easily snap if bent), capable of accepting a maximum of detail, and with the attractive brightness of the original pure tin. The moulds in which flat models were and are still cast today are composed of two slabs of slate – a soft easily workable stone – with the design engraved into one surface on each completely flat and highly polished slab, together with a pouring channel and grooves through which air can escape. Registration 'keys' are also provided, so that the halves of the engraved design match exactly when the two parts of the mould are clamped together ready for the molten metal to be introduced. After this operation has been carried out, and a brief cooling period allowed to elapse, the mould can be opened and the casting extracted ready for cleaning and packing or painting. It is essential that pouring ducts are correctly sized, positioned and cut, in order that metal may flow easily to all parts of the engraving and ensure a full impression, complete in every detail. Since this detail, although often ornate, is cut only shallowly with no undercuts into the mould's surfaces, and the amount of

25

metal per casting is so slight, there is little wear on the design, so that a mould remains efficient even after it has produced large numbers of miniatures. Properly used, with pre-heating before casting, the application of soot or talcum powder to insulate the engraved surfaces, and with storage in warm dry conditions, a slate mould should last indefinitely.

Working, then, with slate moulds and metal alloys suited to their own preferences, the figure manufacturers – principally in Germany but including factories in Austria and Switzerland – built up an industry which brought *Zinnfiguren* to a huge market, and from their initial purpose as playthings has established them as objects of appeal to the serious collector. The variety of subjects depicted over the years has been staggering, including not only the whole kaleidoscope of human life from its earliest times, but also zoological, botanical, architectural, scenic and engineering themes of considerable complexity and great diversity. Among many charming non-military sets there have been those representing country fairs, beer-gardens, the circus, market-places, country festivals and dances, early railways, maritime subjects, hunting scenes and the history of fashion. Themes from classic literature and folk-lore have also been extremely popular, and such exciting subjects as fire-fighters and mediaeval punishments have received due attention from the engravers of *Zinnfiguren*. It would be difficult to find a topic that has not been covered, often in some depth, at some time or another in two-dimensional models; even the space-age has been represented by a set of astronauts in their cumbersome protective suits, complete with surveying gear and shuttle-craft.

As toys, flat figures in the nineteenth and twentieth century were supplied unpainted or ready-finished, and in thin wooden or cardboard boxes, decorated with bright labels and gilt paper. They were sold by weight rather than by numbers, in boxes of two, four and eight ounces, and one pound – the latter containing up to one hundred and fifty pieces which might include scenic accessories or enough items to stage a complete battle in miniature, with maps and accounts of the action provided.

Painting was mostly of a crude but colourful nature which rarely did any kind of justice to the accuracy and intricacy of the basic designs, and was carried on at home by women and children – some as young as six years old – who received very low wages for their work and so kept down prices to the customer. Unpainted figures were of course cheaper still and allowed a certain amount of self-expression to their youthful owners if they wished to apply colours themselves.

However, almost from the date of their introduction, 'flats' were regarded as more than mere toys by a number of adult persons, who saw them as miniature *objets d'art* and preserved them for viewing in glass cabinets. Later still a class of collector developed which used the little figures, massed into military formations, to fight historical actions in a form of table warfare, or to create against suitable scenic backgrounds parade, battle, ceremonial and campaign occasions in miniature. Thus modern war-gamers and diorama constructors had their counterparts in an earlier time.

The study of military history and costume as applied to the correct painting and finishing of models also made big strides towards the end of the nineteenth century and many collectors, inspired by the work of such artists as Frenchmen Paul Armont, Leopold Marchant and Maître Hamel in Paris, achieved results that were more than satisfactory, even judged by the high standards reached in the present day.

Some collectors, interested in periods or types not already covered by commercial castings, began to design and cast their own pieces, and an association of like-minded enthusiasts was formed in Germany for the purpose of furthering the pastime, closely followed by the setting up in Kiel of a company whose production was specifically intended for collectors, with superbly engraved moulds by L. Frank (some of which are still in production for the present proprietor Aloys Ochel, whose firm is probably the largest present-day manufacturer of flats). Many collectors between the two World Wars produced superb designs for series of flat figures,

27

which they either engraved into moulds themselves or had cut for them by quality craftsmen like Ludwig Frank, Sixtus Maier, Bruno Hinsch and Andreas Ferner.

Prominent among collectors and patrons of that inter-war period was a Leipzig fur merchant, Otto Gottstein, who commissioned designs by the best artists available from which Frank engraved moulds. He specialized in dioramic groups, particularly of Ancient Peoples, and achieved remarkable results at the Leipzig exhibition in 1930 – the first such international display of *Zinnfiguren*. When Gottstein emigrated to England in 1933 he took his enthusiasms with him and extended his interest to British history. Fortunately he had kept in contact with his designer friends in Germany, from whom he commissioned the figures which formed the basis for a superb series of fifteen dioramas of incidents and battles from British history (with scenic settings by Denny Stokes) which he presented to the museum of the Royal United Services' Institute in London, where they attracted much admiration and attention for many years. Unfortunately this museum, housed in the great Banqueting Hall at Whitehall, has now closed its doors, but several of the Gottstein dioramas have survived and are on display in other museums of the British Services.

Today's collectors of flats are still mainly concentrated on the continent of Europe, especially in Germany and Austria, although there is a strong and growing body of enthusiasts in Great Britain and the United States of America. One of the very finest painters in this field is the Englishman Jim Woodley, whose work, carried out in artists' oil colours, achieves standards of almost gem-like brilliance. Some of his best pieces are the subjects of plates in the illustrated section of this book and show what superlative results can be obtained by the marriage of excellent designs with inspired painting. Outstanding professional engravers of the calibre of Ludwig Frank, the Sixtus Maiers (father and son), Johannes Frauendorf, Andreas Ferner, Franz Karl Mohr, Georg Rossner, and Hans Lecke have produced, and in the case of the two last-named still produce, designs for collector-standard *Zinnfiguren* of the

28

highest quality and widest range of subjects, fully deserving the attention they receive from serious collectors who carry on in the traditions laid down for over two centuries. Large numbers of amateur designers and engravers contribute to the enormous variety of subjects to which additions are still regularly made.

Zinnfiguren in diorama settings can be seen in museums all over Europe, particularly at the Castle of Kulmbach, where each year a great convention of enthusiasts and manufacturers is held. The little 'tin soldier' can truly be said to have an honoured and vital place as part of the military miniature hobby.

4

The Connoisseur Figure in Metal and Plastic

We have read how the 'toy' soldier industry developed to include flat, solid and hollow-cast *ronde-bosse* or fully modelled subjects in truly comprehensive variety, how improvements in techniques made them available to an ever-widening proportion of the population and how, in the period between the two World Wars, individuals and (adult) enthusiasts or collectors became established, who amassed and in some cases 'converted' or otherwise improved upon the products of commercial manufacturers. These collectors were almost entirely dependent upon 'toy' pieces for their raw materials, and – if any extensive alteration or conversion was to be attempted – had to acquire skills in soldering, engraving, animation and building up varied or additional detail on the commercial castings, plus some facility in painting the results of their conversion efforts to an acceptable degree of realism. Quite a number of enthusiasts were able to develop these skills to a high degree, some indeed created their own figures from scratch, but the majority, for all sorts of reasons, achieved only moderate success in this direction and had to sustain their interest with simple animation and re-painting.

Inevitably, a desire for more detailed and adventurously posed pieces began to manifest itself in the hobby, because (always except-ing the wealth of material available to the collector of *Zinnfiguren*) toy figures tended to be limited both in the amount of engraved detail they incorporated and in their animation, which was, for the most part, representative of stiff 'drill-book' and marching attitudes. In order to meet this demand to some extent, several manufacturers of commercial model figures put out sets that involved a special higher-priced 'collector' standard of painting, and in one or two instances special new castings were issued. The Waterloo line and Highland infantry produced by Britain's in 1937 are cases in point; but such concessions to what was after all a very tiny market were rare and comparatively costly when set against standard toy items.

A small range of mediaeval pieces, outstanding in the high qual-ity of their design and accuracy of their heraldic painting, were produced between the wars by the English artist Robert Cour-tenay, who also issued a limited number of 'personality' figures and ancients. These were welcomed with enthusiasm by the collecting fraternity, who were also treated to several excellent designs by William Carman, but except for the exquisite 'bespoke' pieces produced by a few French miniaturists like Marcel Baldet, Berdou, Metayer and Josianne Desfontaines, collectors were not well catered for until the expansion of interest in the hobby immediately following World War II, when gifted designers began to produce models specifically to meet collectors' demands.

Such figures were not intended in any way to be toys, and because they were not subjected to the wear and tear of 'play', they could be made to accommodate delicacy of pose with fineness of uniform, equipment and weapon detail of a very high standard indeed. Almost without exception 'connoisseur' figures in the early days were metal castings, sometimes offered as kits of parts to be finished by the purchaser, sometimes assembled but unpainted, and more rarely sold as completely finished miniatures ready for the collectors' cabinets.

Contributing to the spread of interest in connoisseur pieces and the rapidity with which comprehensive ranges were built up was the adaptation of centrifugal casting in vulcanized rubber moulds to the processes of production, enabling models to be turned out quickly and cheaply with high-definition of embossed and engraved detail. Rubber moulds, compared with the traditional bronze or steel types, can be made easily as well as at reasonable cost, can permit a degree of undercutting in the design of 'master' figures, and because of their flexibility can cope with a greater degree of animation in the piece. With proper use, sufficient castings can be obtained from a rubber mould to make it a sound economic proposition, while the same 'master' can be used over and over again in the making of identical moulds where really long production runs are required. Although some designers prefer simple 'drop' casting, that is, pouring molten metal into a static mould, the centrifuge remains today the principal method of turning out connoisseur miniatures.

It is generally accepted that the artist more responsible than any other for establishing the high-quality collector figure was Charles Stadden, who commenced his production in 1951 and was associated soon afterwards with the British company Norman Newton Ltd, now Tradition. He brought his superb craftsmanship to the creation of an enormous range of subjects, the majority in 'standard' 54mm scale. Over the years the Stadden range has become renowned world-wide for the accuracy and vivacity of its component figures, and the master craftsman has worked in other scales, smaller and larger than 'standard', with equal facility. Of late, operating his own company, Stadden has been producing splendid large-scale figures in polished pewter. Where Stadden led, other artists and sculptors were not slow to follow. Outstanding designs were and still are produced by Russell Gammage of Rose Models, Major Bob Rowe of Ensign Miniatures, Tim Richards of Phoenix

Models, John Tassel, Malcolm Dawson, Edward Suren, Cliff Sanderson, Roger Saunders, Frank Hinchliffe, Ray Lamb, John Jenkinson, Al Charles, Brian Owen, Ronald Cameron, Bill Hearne, Sid Horton and Marcus Hinton, among many others in the United Kingdom.

In addition there are numbers of collectors who produce designs of high quality and from them cast short runs of figures for their own private use. There are in the United States of America similar talented miniaturists: Alan Silk, Sheperd Paine, the Imrie/Risley partnership, Jack Scruby, another Ray Lamb, Cy Broman, Bill Murray and so many more, including the Englishman Pat Bird, now settled in California, whose 'Series 77' figurines have justly earned great approval. On the continent of Europe, Jose Amiral, Signor Parisini and other gifted designers are responsible for metal collector-figure ranges of great interest and merit, and, particularly in Italy, the 54mm miniature has reached a high level of sophistication. Inevitably, many excellent figure-makers have not been mentioned, but no discourtesy is intended; indeed this work pays tribute to all who contribute to the wealth of material available to today's collectors. Metal connoisseur figures – in the general high quality of their designs and the comprehensiveness of their subject coverage – are going a very long way towards providing even the most exacting enthusiast with miniatures that can be welcomed into a collection with confidence and satisfaction.

Because there is less need to correct detail or stance in the modern metal figure, and because, although reasonably priced, they are much more expensive than the metal toy figures of days gone by, there is not so much major conversion of this type of model. In the larger scales conversion is almost unknown, the modeller's work being confined to detailing and painting for the most part, since considerations of space argue against dioramic settings and multiple groupings of these giants of the model world. However, because of the additional scope for intricate detail of clothing, accoutrements and weapons afforded by representation in large scale, there is a very definite tendency towards the 'big-boys' by

33

collectors whose interests are less involved with impressions of movement, action and re-action within an environment.

Connoisseur figures are not confined to metal castings by any means. This is an age in which plastics have been developed and are employed in ever more diverse aspects of daily life. So versatile are these materials that they can be said to rival metals in strength and endurance, while having many properties that more traditional materials lack. Although several types of plastic are used in the production of toy figures, it is the rigid type which provides the medium for connoisseur pieces, principally polystyrene, a material which is moulded by the pressure injection system, requiring expensive and complicated machines.

It follows that figures need to be produced in some quantity to make them commercially viable, and this in turn means that an efficient distribution and marketing organization is required for their presentation to the customer. However, provided the numbers can be made and disposed of satisfactorily enough to keep prices within reasonable limits, plastic models have several not inconsiderable advantages. The material is admirably suited to the retention of the most elaborate detail, and because it is forced into the mould under pressure it will allow the tiniest of shapes to be incorporated into a design. It is easily worked with the simplest of tools, can be bonded and welded with a variety of agents and presents a smooth, chemically inert surface which will readily accept most water, oil and enamel based paints. Produced for the most part in 'high-impact' varieties, hard plastics are not unduly brittle, have sufficient rigidity to allow the moulding of thin sections without drooping, and do not deteriorate under the influences of time and atmospheric content. Fine detail is, however, rather fragile, and the handling of completed models should be kept to an absolute minimum in order to avoid damage.

So widely used are plastics in the field of military miniatures today, and so excellent the results achieved by professional and amateur alike, that it seems strange to realize that only a decade or so ago there was a great deal of reluctance on the part of enthusiasts to accept plastic connoisseur figures, even though many early designs showed artistic merit of a high order. Objections were made to the new materials on grounds of weight, 'feel', durability and so on, but as their undoubted advantages became more apparent, and more and more quality pieces were produced by sculptors and engravers of solid reputations, resistance slackened, and plastic models now stand on an equal footing with those made in more traditional media.

Complete figures are produced in hard plastic, prominent among them being the ranges issued by Mokarex, Starluxe, Elastolin and Preisser, but it is in the realm of assembly kits that the majority of connoisseur pieces are to be found. Since even the most complex poses, and extravagant details of clothing and equipment, can be captured by carefully cementing together a number of component parts, modellers of all standards find plastic figure assembly kits both convenient and satisfying.

Those individuals with the imagination and skills to do so can inter-mix and combine parts from any number of kits (provided they are to the same scale) in the creation of new designs, and the materials are so tractable that actual alteration or 'conversion' is possible with only simple tools and techniques. There is in fact virtually no limit to the scope for ingenuity and flair that is offered to the figure modeller by hard plastic models, whether of figures, vehicles, weapons or other accessories; and the cost is usually reasonable, even modest.

Among the leading manufacturers of hard plastic figure assembly kits are Historex, with designs by Leliepvre, Airfix (for whom Ronald Cameron sculpts many of the 'masters'), Almark, whose ranges – now unfortunately discontinued – were modelled by Charles Stadden, E.S.C.I. (featuring work by Bill Hearne), and Heller in France, Tamiya in Japan, Monogram in the United States, and Italieri in Italy, all of whom produce designs by artists and sculptors of great skill and imagination. So far, the majority of pieces seem to be of Napoleonic and World War II subjects, but there are other subjects and there will undoubtedly be more, enlarging on present ranges and branching out into new areas of interest – an example being the exquisitely detailed series of Samurai figures now available from Tamiya.

Since there is, as far as I am aware, no way by which polystyrene can be adapted for home-casting (the injection-moulding procedure being essentially a commercial proposition), original work by enthusiasts is almost entirely achieved, on the figure side at least, by 'conversion' and 'scratch-building'. So imaginative and technically adept are the leading modellers of today, however, that the work they turn out by these processes falls quite definitely into the category of original creation, with other materials and substances being employed, in many cases, in addition to the basic plastic components (which themselves are subjected to alteration). Many examples of such exquisite conversion work are illustrated among the colour plates in this volume. Connoisseur figures today, whether metal or plastic, original or conversion, have achieved a general standard of excellence which establishes them as true *objets d'art*, and their creators as artists worthy of the highest praise and distinction.

5

Model Soldiers Today
A Review

It must by now have become quite plain to the reader of this volume that military miniatures of one kind or another exist today in an almost bewildering variety of types and subjects, covering the whole spectrum of service life and a fair proportion of civilian pursuits in addition. So multitudinous are the pieces available, whether as toys, assembly kits or connoisseur models, unpainted or completely finished, that anyone starting out in the hobby could be stricken with indecision over the precise course to follow, even when the general direction is known – the collection of toy figures, scenic groups, representation of historical events or costume, or whatever.

In such an event it may be useful to the individual to establish a theme for his or her collection and keep within its boundaries when buying, converting, or building component pieces from scratch. Or, a collection can be made up of whatever takes the modeller's fancy with no overall pattern. Both methods are equally valid, and each has advantages and disadvantages; it is the amount of enjoyment and satisfaction that can be derived from the hobby that counts.

Whatever course is adopted, consideration will need to be given to questions of space available for housing a collection, finance for its acquisition and maintenance, what can be obtained in ready-made designs, and what needs to be produced by the collector himself either by conversion or 'scratch-building'. Even the interested observer who does not himself collect will find it useful to know just what he is looking at, the better to appreciate its qualities and understand the skills that have been involved in its production.

As we learned in previous chapters, models today are made principally in metal or plastic, and come ready for painting or as assembly kits. There are small numbers of completely finished pieces available as stock 'bespoke' items, and some are made from unusual materials, wood, resin, plaster and plasticene among them; overwhelmingly, however, connoisseur figures as purchased require some work on the part of the modeller to bring them to a finished state. This means that, in part at least, each completed model is different from all the others produced from the same mould, and allows an individual collector to develop a distinct style. Therein lies much of the charm of the hobby, and, as can be appreciated from our colour plates, the uses to which commercial models can be put, and the variations in colour, attitude and embellishment that can be incorporated into their final presentation can be quite staggering.

Apart from subject, one of the most pertinent factors affecting the choice of a particular model is its scale. This is expressed as a formula, e.g., 9mm to the foot, indicating that every foot of real measurement is represented by 9mm in the model; or as a fraction, e.g., 1/24th, which means that the prototype's dimensions are twenty-four times as great as those of the model. Pieces can also be described in terms of their actual size as in the case of a '54mm' figure which equals 9mm to the foot for a model of a man who would really be 6ft tall. There are a number of internationally accepted scales, to which the vast majority of military miniatures are designed: the larger embracing what are virtually statuettes and the smaller including pieces used in wargaming and 'micro' modelling. The principal military modelling scales, and the kinds of models that can be found within them, are:

90mm, or 1/20th or 15mm to the foot. A scale which permits the most intricate detail to be incorporated into the design of a model, whatever its subject, and a favourite of the eminent sculptors Charles Stadden, Ronald Cameron and Ray Lamb. There are also several limited ranges of plastic assembly kits of vehicles and artillery made in this scale. It does, however, involve problems for the painter, whose work needs to be very subtly carried out if the best results are to be achieved and a 'doll-like' effect avoided. Most 90mm pieces are made in metal.

77mm, or 1/24th, or 13mm to the foot. Increasingly popular among enthusiasts who require super-detailing and scope for painting, this scale is represented in the lists of most major manufacturers of connoisseur figures and equipment. Ranges of subjects are constantly being expanded and – like the previous category – the majority are cast in metal.

54mm, or 1/32nd, or 9mm to the foot. This is the classic model soldier scale in which vast numbers of toy, and connoisseur pieces have been designed since its establishment as No. 1 Railway Gauge in the closing years of the last century. Large enough to accommodate a considerable degree of detail, it is not over-demanding in its requirements for display space, and is equally popular with modellers of figures and vehicles, etc. Without doubt the greater part of all military modelling work is done in this scale; it is the most familiar to enthusiast and casual observer alike, and it attracts the attention of the very finest designers, both professional and amateur. As a general-purpose scale for all types of miniature work, including scenic settings, '54mm' approaches the ideal, and it is firmly established as the 'standard' although, in practice, pieces nominally 54mm may vary from 52 to 57mm or slightly larger, say 1/35th to 1/30th in fractions, or between 8.5 to 10mm to the foot. This is the scale that comes to mind when model soldiers are mentioned, and it includes metal and plastics among its base media.

40mm–42mm, or 1/48th–1/43rd, or 7mm to the foot. Another very popular scale in which can be found figures, vehicles and equipment of many kinds, including aircraft and trains ('O' Gauge). Although less comprehensive as far as subject range is concerned than the 54mm scale, it nonetheless permits almost as much detail to be incorporated into a model, and has advantages if display space is limited. On the whole more favoured by enthusiasts for trains, aircraft and vehicles than by figure collectors.

30mm, or 1/60th, or 5mm to the foot. This 'standard' scale for *Zinnfiguren* or flats has also attracted several first-class designers of *ronde-bosse* pieces whose work is particularly lively and imaginative. Edward Suren's 'Willie' figures are excellent examples of this kind of work, with an amazing amount of detail incorporated into each model. Particularly suitable for dioramas and scenic groups involving numbers of pieces, this scale also includes war-games models and collector-type items.

25mm, or 1/76th–1/72nd, or 4mm to the foot. Important to the figure modeller who wishes to depict large numbers of troops in ceremonial or campaign situations, but primarily for the collector of miniature vehicles and aircraft, this is sometimes known as 'one-inch' scale. It is also, of course, a popular scale with wargamers (as is its next in line, *20mm, or 1/86th–1/90th or 3.5mm to the foot*).

Pieces made to smaller scales than the ones shown above, without decrying them in any way, are not 'model soldiers' in the accepted sense, but wargaming items or symbols. Similarly, models larger than 90mm are more properly described as statuettes or mannikins, and again lie outside the true model soldier classification. (Some specimens of large-scale figures are included in our colour plates, however, to demonstrate the very high standards of artistry and technique that are achieved by the masters in this exacting branch of military miniaturization.)

From all that has been said so far in this chapter it will be apparent that the contemporary model soldier enthusiast has opportunities unequalled in any former period to indulge his interests in whatever specialist direction they may lie. Not only is there more available in the way of models – both in kit form and ready-assembled – but veritable floods of reference data, background material, and guidance in the acquisition of skills and techniques can be obtained readily and at reasonable cost. In recent years a vigorous modelling press has grown up, with magazines and periodicals devoted to specialized subjects within the hobby and providing a constant stream of useful information, often supplied by well-known modellers who give advice, solve problems and suggest suitable projects. Several such periodicals maintain correspondence columns in which ideas and comments can be exchanged, and the extent to which they are filled is an indication of the enthusiasm and genuine thirst for knowledge that exists within the hobby.

Reference material is being made available in ever-increasing quantitites in the museums and institutions dealing with military matters, so that rare books, photographs and prints can be consulted to establish details of dress and equipment in a way not possible in earlier times. Often copies of such items can be had at very low cost, and the staff of such establishments are almost invariably eager to give maximum assistance. So much in the way of authentic documentation is accessible that there is less and less excuse nowadays for manufacturers or modellers to get wrong any specific aspect of their miniatures. Of course there *are* areas in which reliable information is scarce, but these present a challenge to the researcher, rather than insuperable obstacles.

Perhaps the most abundant sources of encouragement and stimulation for modellers can be found in the specialist societies which have been formed over the past forty years or so. Within these

41

organizations like-minded enthusiasts can exchange information and techniques, test and develop their skills by competition and display, and be of general mutual assistance in the furtherance of their hobby. Societies and clubs exist and flourish throughout Europe, the Americas and Australasia, with members, if not formed groups, in many other parts of the globe. Many produce their own journals, hold regular meetings, foster competitions, support displays and provide platforms for the wider dissemination of information and techniques. The British Model Soldier Society, which claims to be the most senior group of its kind in the world, holds its Annual Competitions in London, an event which enjoys an international reputation for the highest standards of workmanship and imaginative presentation of models. A similar event is held each year at Chester in Pennsylvania, attracting competitors from many areas of the United States and other countries.

Meetings such as these provide opportunities for enthusiasts of all standards of competence to match their skills one against another and to discuss their abilities and techniques to the benefit of all concerned. Thus fresh ideas are spread, friendships are formed and renewed, and the hobby is strengthened and revitalized by the interchange of thought and experience.

Military miniatures today can be seen to afford opportunities for artistic creativity, interest in historical events, costume, national sense and effective research, as well as for the pursuit of strictly military matters. The hobby encourages the development of techniques for working in metals, plastics and a multitude of other materials, painting in various media, and the construction of realistic environmental settings, at the same time imposing those artistic disciplines necessary to the production of accurate, convincing models. Its devotees can work in several different but internationally acceptable scales, and have an enormous wealth of reference aids, tools and finishes to help them make the most of the legions of figures and assembly kits available for their choice. Advice and instruction are provided by societies, clubs and magazines so that a beginner need never feel that he is operating in a vacuum, and, above all, the subject itself offers so much scope for representation of types and events from the age of the stone axe to that of the nuclear missile. Yes, it is indeed a far cry from the days when a budding collector, on his own or at best as a member of a very small group, would have to do the best job he could with the toy figures that were the only basic pieces available. Today a whole industry caters for his requirements and seeks to anticipate his future interests.

6

Guns, Vehicles, Equipment and Display

Because of their possibilities for the depiction of weapons, vehicles, ancillary equipment and, where relevant, animals, as well as the personnel of gun detachments and command units, artillery subjects are very popular among modellers, and are well represented in the lists of manufacturers of toy, collector and wargaming items. Some of the best feature among the 54mm range produced by the English firm Hinchliffe Models, who also make one or two larger-scale pieces, and other excellent examples are sold, mostly in kit form, by Imrie/Risley, Superior Models and H-R Products in the United States, Tamiya of Japan, Historex, E.S.C.I. and Italieri on the Continent, and Blenheim, Trophy and Mark Time in the United Kingdom.

It is possible to give a very good impression of artillery on parade or in action from standard stock items, but there is plenty of room for the modeller to add his own personal touch by scratch-building such equipment as battery boards, plotting tables, telephone equipment, ammunition replenishment systems, and so on. Guns are strong, functional machines, evocative of great power and purpose, and make ideal subjects for diorama work, along with their associated limbers, tractors and directing paraphernalia. Most attractive, too, are models of the various animals employed in bygone days to transport guns and bring them into and out of action, particularly teams of horses, which offer a real challenge in the correct depiction of animal classification and harness type (the latter varied so much between one period or nation and another that careful research is necessary to establish the exact details).

For the mechanically-minded there is great satisfaction to be obtained from representing the huge variety of prime-movers, tracked and wheeled, that have replaced animal teams in this century, and the self-propelled equipments that are typical of the artillery scene in the present day. Although lacking the picturesque qualities of animal-drawn guns, these machines are impressive enough in their own right, presenting with their detachments, whether on parade or campaign, some of the more awesome aspects of modern military hardware.

As an obvious focus for attack or defence, artillery has featured in spectacular situations in many battles of the past, when to capture an enemy's guns was often a prime object of a general's tactics, while to lose his own ordnance to an opponent amounted to humiliating disgrace. Guns were particularly desirable trophies of war, and in their successful conquest or protection deeds of heroism have been perpetrated that make ideal themes for modelling, especially effective when presented in dioramic form. The subject is immensely varied, with the guns themselves – varying from the primitive mediaeval bombard to the mighty atomic cannon of the present era – offering to the modeller unlimited opportunities for imaginative portrayal. Miniature engineering, in which precision and technical skills of many kinds are involved, has often taken the gun in one form or another as the subject for some of its best manifestations. Even in model form, artillery can firmly convince the observer of its role as 'the ultimate argument of kings'.

No less varied, and equally interesting, is the enormous range of transportation by which armies throughout the ages enabled themselves to move personnel, equipment and supplies. There are severe limitations on the size and weight of items that can be carried on the backs of men or animals, so to cope with the quantities needed to keep even a modest force in the field for any length of time it is necessary to have efficient load-carrying vehicles in support. Initially adopting and adapting civilian vehicles for their requirements, armies gradually developed specialist types better suited to the demands and exigencies of military service.

During the nineteenth century a considerable degree of sophistication and efficiency distinguished military transportation, which, relying as it did upon animals of one kind and another for its tractive power, needed to combine a minimum of vehicle weight with a maximum of strength and capacity. In the British Army, by the latter half of the century, animal-drawn vehicles had become capable of carrying no less than twice their own unladen weight behind teams of two, four or more animals (depending upon the condition of the countries and roads that had to be travelled). In most other armies of a regular or established nature a more or less similar efficiency had been achieved.

The portrayal of animal-draught military vehicles can be attractive to the modeller, combining as it does requirements for techniques in producing convincing animals as well as straightforward carriages of various kinds. These last, although designed for many different purposes and of diverse shapes, are rarely of a very complex nature from the point of view of construction. In almost every case manufacturers of commercial toy soldier ranges included animal transport vehicles in their lists, ambulances and waggons being particularly prominent; and the models were generally reasonable scale replicas of their prototypes. Connoisseur figure makers, probably on grounds of cost, have produced much less in this line, but occasionally examples turn up. Some assembly kit manufacturers are more prolific in this respect – excellent examples in cast metal coming from firms like Phoenix, while Historex offer delightful ambulances, field-forges, caissons and waggons.

It is fortunate that animal-draught vehicles are not over-complicated in design, since this means that modellers of average ability can quite easily produce their own items from scratch, using the many scale-drawings that are available as guides and utilizing standard materials such as balsa wood, sheet, strip rod, 'sectioned' plastic, and so on. Only wheels are likely to present much difficulty and these can often be obtained as spares from kit manufacturers or firms specializing in accessories. Museums such as the National Army Museum and Imperial War Museum in London, the Musée de l'Armée in Paris, and many others, have numbers of excellent animal-drawn military vehicle models on display, which serve admirably as guides to scratch-builders, and it is still possible to find actual, well-preserved vehicles at regimental and corps depots, army displays and gatherings of vehicle enthusiasts.

Only some seventy years or so have elapsed since the general introduction of mechanically propelled vehicles into military service. Before that time there had been limited employment of steam-engined types, but the practical application of the internal combustion engine to the propulsion of load-carriers was the real turning point. Wheeled and tracked suspensions were involved almost from the start, and purpose-built combat machines, armoured fighting vehicles, made their appearance as practical propositions, during World War I. Motor transport was soon capable of undertaking all the tasks for which animal-draught types had become adapted and led to the development of even more specialization, some catering for the needs of the vehicles, while others made the most of power sources to drive generators, cranes, winches and other machinery which was built as an integral part of the motor bodies. Eventually, although it took many years because of the natural conservatism of the military outlook and the parsimony of most political administrations, mechanical transport took over the field completely, and animals, mercifully, were no longer required for military service, except in a limited ceremonial capacity.

The modelling world is well served for replicas of military motor vehicles, armoured and soft-skin alike. Assembly-kit manufacturers produce wide ranges in several standard scales, and there is a steady stream of new items. Many of the world's leading modellers produce some of their best work when combining model vehicles with miniature figures, as a glance at our plates showing examples of the output of Shep Paine, François Verlinden and others will confirm, and at least one international society has been formed to cater solely for the interests of miniature-vehicle modellers. Certainly, this aspect of the hobby has no lack of keen participants, of whom a significant proportion make up their models from scratch or carry out extensive conversions on commercial assembly kits. The real military world has become ever more technical and comprehensive in its employment of machines, vehicles and equipment, and the world of miniatures keeps in step with it, pace by pace.

Where a collection includes models of men, animals, guns and vehicles, it is best if a common scale is used for them all, or, at least, if items displayed together are the same scale. This allows an observer to get a much more accurate impression from the models of the relative sizes and bulk of the real objects. For example, the Sherman tank was a massive machine weighing over thirty tons and of an overall height of 9ft. Even in 1/32nd scale it can look very impressive, but with a 1/24th human figure alongside, it loses a great deal of impact, and with a 1/72nd figure it seems grotesquely gigantic. Only a 1/32nd figure in such a situation would convey the true relative proportions of man to machine. The same-scale principle does not *have* to apply to a collection, but in my opinion it adds to the impression of realism that can be conveyed by any group of models.

Where scenic settings are concerned, the purposes of realism can only be served by a correct-scale relationship between all the pieces making up such a presentation. In cased dioramas, which seek to give an illusion of distance and perspective, they may, admittedly, be a mixture of scales, but even in these instances items supposed to be at similar distances from the observer must be in the same scale.

It is the function of a scenic setting to create the appearance of reality, for just as real people exist in an environment, so models of them become more convincing if set in a model environment. The proposition seems obvious enough, and it is true that much of the most effective modelling done today involves some degree of scenic work. Even single figures, whatever their scales, are the better for a little groundwork on their bases.

Many of the colour plates in this book show models in an environment or photographed against a scenic background, and the added realistic impact that they gain from this treatment is readily apparent. However, it must also be clear that to display the modelling subjects to their best advantage the scenic elements must themselves be constructed with skill and perception. A scrap or two of dyed lichen and some green flock powder glued on to a cardboard sheet are no longer acceptable as representations of a hedge and grassy meadow, although not so long ago they might well have been hailed with enthusiasm as the acme of realism!

The tendency nowadays is to utilize all sorts of 'natural' items – mosses, grasses, twigs, roots, stones, and so on – to represent the natural elements in scenic settings; it is a question of form and texture. What, after all, can represent a plant in miniature better than a miniature plant? Thus the delicate branches and foliage of various mosses, particularly the spaghnum varieties, present in miniature much of the appearance of a full-sized hedge or under-growth, and similarly the root system of an ash seedling, dried and 'up-ended', is amazingly like the branch system of a young tree! Rock textures are best conveyed by rock, earth by real dirt or sand, and vegetation of all kinds by the tiny plants to be found in garden and countryside. Fabricated scenic features – bridges, buildings, fortifications, etc. – must be treated in miniature as models in their own right, and should be constructed with care to convey as much of an impression of the real thing as is consistent with the builder's skills and materials to hand.

Having made this point, it should be stressed that to be successful, a scenic setting should not overpower the modelling subject for which it serves as an environment; a nice balance should be maintained. Our illustrations show many examples of scenic

49

work of a very high standard, and demonstrate what can be achieved in the realistic presentation of many kinds of model subjects. A painter creates, by means of colours and textures on a flat surface, the illusion of real three-dimensional forms and distances. It is the object of the scenic modeller to create similar impressions in the mind of the beholder by the skilful disposition of his scraps of painted metal and plastic, moss, sand and stone.

7

Conversion and Scratch-building

No work covering the military miniature hobby should fail to mention the arts of conversion and scratch-building, for it is in these areas that many of the imaginative concepts that give the pastime so much of its charm and impact are to be found. This is not to detract in any way from the skills and artistry of the original designers of commercial figures, since it is upon the basic accuracy of their interpretations of anatomy and proportion that the converter, in particular, relies to a very great extent. But commercial pieces are produced in quantity – all alike for any given design – and without subsequent re-working other than painting they allow an enthusiast little scope to develop an individual style. Some modellers are content with this and put what they can of their characteristics into finishing the commercial piece as well as their skills permit, but a very significant proportion use the products of a manufacturer as the raw material, as it were, for their own ideas of pose and dress; others again create figures from scratch, just as a commercial designer would do, and turn out work that is unique and 'personalized'. It can therefore be said that in these aspects of modelling imaginative and creative talents can be employed to their fullest extent.

'Conversion' in modelling terms means alteration, and covers the re-working of basic commercial items from a simple change of limb position to a complete re-arrangement of pose, uniform or proportion. It may fairly be asked why, in view of the huge amount of material available, it is necessary or desirable to bother with conversion, which is practised both as a remedial measure and as a means of exercising creativity. In the first case, the converter is seeking to put right faults of dimension, proportion, posture or detail which may be present in a commercial design by reason of mould requirements and limitations, and by doing so make the piece more accurate and convincing than it would otherwise have been. In the second instance, he would be striving for variety of stance, dress or equipment, and to arrive at a model unique to his own collection or production. There can, of course, be good reasons for both types of conversion work on the same model.

Quite clearly, if a modeller is to put right a commercial design, or change it into something radically different, he must know what the faults are and how to rectify them and, further, what is accurate and correct for any new piece that he wishes to represent. In addition he must have mastered the techniques that are necessary in carrying out his intentions and have available whatever tools and materials are required. To get the best results a converter must master the skills involved in his work, and be able to understand and translate into practical form those factors of anatomical pose, uniform detail, technical and mechanical data relative to the subject with which he is dealing.

Living creatures – human beings and animals of all kinds – probably pose the most problems, and some understanding of their basic anatomy and how their forms change under the influences of movement and the restrictions imposed by dress, equipment and environment is essential if they are to be represented acceptably in model form. Although not themselves able to move like their prototypes, models are often required to *suggest* movement by means of a pose that captures the essence of a complete action, and the more fully he understands the functioning of a creature's anatomy, in terms of shape, proportion and balance, the better will the converter be able to select that particular pose. Only by knowing the capabilities and limitations of anatomical structure will the modeller avoid producing figures in poses and with conformations which would be grotesque or impossible to achieve in real life.

Fortunately, particularly in the case of the human form, we have no lack of a wide variety of examples, surrounded, as most of us are on even a short walk down the nearest High Street, with living specimens of different builds, ages, genders, and even colours. Nonetheless, anatomical proportions do conform to certain rules, and any failure to comply with them is instantly conspicuous. An authoritative book on artistic anatomy is therefore a very definite asset on the bookshelf of the serious converter and scratch-builder; properly used it could be invaluable. Most public library services are able to provide textbooks on anatomy, human and animal.

Obviously, it will be artistic anatomy – i.e., articulation, musculature and proportion – with which a modeller will be concerned, there being no requirement in his art for specialized knowledge of the internal structure and organs. Two of the best practical volumes for sculptors and modellers are *The Human Figure in Motion* and *Animals in Motion*, both by Eadweard Muybridge, a noted Victorian photographer, and containing hundreds of examples of everyday actions and attitudes, many taken simultaneously from several aspects. Though they are not inexpensive these books are a very sound investment for any modeller, providing a wealth of practical information, which – although prepared nearly a hundred years ago with cumbersome camera and technical equipment – has in my opinion never been surpassed.

As well as modelling properly proportioned figures of men and beasts, converters need to represent clothing and equipment for those figures as accurately and realistically as possible. This requires some knowledge of military and civil costume and harness for the relevant period, with an understanding of the ways in which it was worn, its appearance under varying conditions – such as parade or campaign – and similar comprehension of weapons, equipment and trappings. In the same way, the whole scope of military technology – 'hardware' as the American phrase has it – has undergone enormous changes, especially since the introduction of rifle and breech-loading artillery, smokeless powder, the invention of the internal combustion engine (which has made possible self-propelled fighting and transport vehicles), aircraft and all sorts of other marvels of engineering and mechanics.

The high standards of accuracy now achieved by leading converters and scratch-builders have been made possible, in part, by the very wide range of information on military subjects which is available in books and periodicals (some specifically devoted to modelling, others of a more general character), prints, photographs, postcards, and so on. The gathering of such data as it applies to a particular project can be a most pleasurable activity, and the building up of a comprehensive (reference) library is both rewarding and utilitarian. So much good-quality material is available to the enthusiast at the present time that there is little excuse for inaccuracy of detail in his modelling presentations, and it is the degree to which this data can be interpreted and combined with imaginative presentation that determines his success.

Perhaps the most valuable attribute in conversion and scratch-building is an ability to visualize the finished piece before work on it even commences. By asking himself three basic questions, as they apply to his project, and establishing the answers in his mind, a modeller can translate his idea more easily into actuality. First, he should ask himself what the model is intended to represent, in what scale, and in what, if any, environment. Then, how much of it can be adopted or adapted from existing models or materials and how much needs to be fabricated. Third, what skills and techniques need to be exercised to turn concept and available material into the completed work. With experience in realizing projects, meeting their challenges and solving the problems encountered during the various stages towards their completion, an ability is developed to tackle more and more ambitious subjects with confidence, and to

54

produce results that are not only pleasing and accurate but also reveal the characteristics of individual style.

An important factor in the successful presentation of any conversion or scratch-building work is the competence with which painting is effected, since this is the process which must convince the observer that he is looking at all the textures – such as cloth, metal, flesh, hide, etc. – that are present in the prototype but are in fact quite different materials in the model. Painting is so influential in its effect that, if well carried out, it can transform quite an ordinary piece into something outstanding; if badly done, it can make even a brilliantly designed and constructed model appear clumsy and amateurish.

Broadly speaking, painting of models divides itself into two principal categories: the 'glossy' and the 'matt' or realistic finish. As the term implies, 'glossy' paints give a hard shiny appearance, resistant to moderate knocks and handling, and are usually employed on pieces in the 'toy' category, wargaming items, and models which are intended to resemble ceramics. In the 'realistic' category all types of textures from high gloss to dead flat are simulated to produce an appearance as close to real life as can be achieved. Both styles have their advantages and advocates, and have, by and large, become associated if not entirely confined to the types of modelling mentioned above. Shiny finishes are obtained by the use of gloss enamel and cellulose paints, or by applying glossy varnishes to cover 'flat' paints. Into the realistic category can be grouped, as well as the 'shinies', matt enamels, oil-bound or water-based poster colours, casein and acrylic colours, gouaches, water-colours, artists' oils, and inks of various kinds. In some cases paints with similar base media are intermixable, thus enabling a wider range of tones and effects to be obtained, but water- and oil-based paints will not mix and cellulose colours can only be used on their own. In order to achieve the best results, only brushes of the highest quality are normally used by top-class painters, but these, although expensive initially, will (if properly used and looked after) give surprisingly long service.

Painting styles vary from modeller to modeller, and most of the acknowledged leaders in the field can readily be identified by the marked individual characteristics of their work (as the reader who studies the colour illustrations in this book will be able to verify). Some of the more subtle effects of light, shade and texture that turn models into miniature masterpieces are, of course, the products of much experimentation and experience, but the standard of painting that is seen in world-wide competitions is extraordinarily high, and seemingly destined to show improvement year by year. Modelling societies quite rightly lay great emphasis on competent painting abilities, and do much by example and instruction to assist their members to improve their styles; and articles in journals devoted to the hobby provide advice and guidance on painting materials and techniques which will enable even a novice to achieve creditable results.

Since painting is the process by which a model is helped to convey an impression of life, it can be argued that it is a form of conversion in itself, and that modellers who carry out no other work than painting commercially produced figures can be termed converters because their use of colours 'converts' the plain plastic or metal into a semblance of flesh, cloth and so on. Certainly very different impressions will be conveyed by identical basic figures which have received treatment from different painters. The correctness of such an argument could be discussed at length; suffice it to say that whatever other skills he may display, the successful converter/scratch-builder will undoubtedly be a painter of competence.

Much of what has been said so far about figures, i.e., representations of living creatures, applies equally to models of vehicles, guns, equipment, architecture and scenic detail, and it is probable that more scratch-building is done in these areas than in figure work. Conversion, too, is frequently resorted to in vehicle modelling, where kits of parts are subjected to much the same modification and adaptation in miniature as was carried out on their full-scale counterparts. Much imaginative and sensitive work

56

emerges from the model 'engineering' aspects of the hobby, often with the relationship between man and machine very forcibly handled.

Military practice is, we are told, both an art and a science; military miniatures at their best reflect both aspects, and allow full scope to both the artistic and technical-minded of their practitioners.

Colour Plates

1 Early Britain's Cavalry.

2 Britain's C.I.V. Ambulance.

3   Heyde Ambulance Waggon.

4   Mignot Infantry.

5   B. Minot: Indian Mountain Artillery.

6   Another view of the same piece.

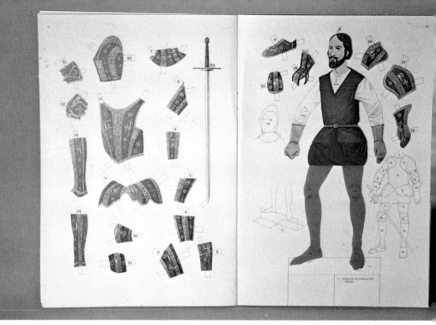

7   Wolfe Publishing: Paper Cut-out Figure.

8   B. Minot: British Infantry Muleteer.

9 Rose Models: Cretan Bull Dancers.

10 Wolfe Publishing: Paper Cut-out Figures.

11   Ensign Miniatures: British Mess-kit c. 1900.

12   Ensign Miniatures: Highlanders 1815.

13　Rose Models: Egyptian Chariot.

14　C. Stadden: Redcoat and Redskin.

15   C. Stadden: British Square at Waterloo.

16   C. Stadden: Burning the Flags, Diorama.

17 Flight Deck of a Space-ship.

18 Series 77: Weapons Collection, 150mm scale.

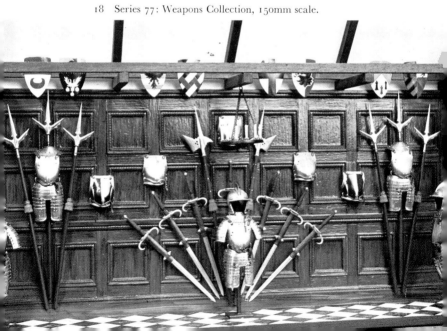

19   Series 77: English Civil War Types.

20   Series 77: Ancient Greeks.

21   Greenwood and Ball: Sudan War Figures 1898.

22   Imrie/Risley: German Paratroops, World War II.

23   Imrie/Risley: Cavalry in the
South-west.

24   J. Tassel: North British Dragoon. 130mm figure.

25   R. Saunders: U.S. Marines.

26 Realmodels: Scout in the
Indian Wars.

27 Sanderson/Caton/Saunders: Victorian Group.

28 Imrie/Risley: Chasseur of the Garde.

29 New Hope Design: Landsknechts.

30 Rose Models: Napoleonic Infantry in Egypt.

31   Rose Models: Persian Immortals.

32   Greenwood and Ball: U.S. Indian Wars Types.

33 Airfix Products: Vehicle Diorama 1942.

34 Airfix Products: 8th Army Group.

35   Airfix Products: Afrika Korps 1943.

36   Hinchliffe Models: Gatling-gun and Detachment.

37 Squadron/Rubin: Moonmaid.

38 Historex: Cuirassier.

39 Historex: Napoleonic Lancer.

40 Phoenix Models: Atlantis Fantasy Scene.

41 J. Woodley: Various
Ancient Types.

42 J. Woodley: A Mix-
ture of Subjects.

43 R. Riehn: Hussar of Frederick the Great.

44 R. Riehn: Review at Potsdam.

R. Riehn: Staff
Conference.

46 R. Riehn: Mounted Officer, time of Frederick the Great.

J. McGerr: Plains Indians.

48 J. Woodley: Display of Exotic Animals.

49 J. Woodley: A Roman Feast.

50 J. Woodley: Egyptian Court Scenes.

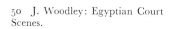

51   D. Catley: Moghul Procession.

52   R. Dilley: M5 Half-track in N.W. Europe 1944.

53   R. Dilley: Near Kalemyo.

54   J. Burn: Rhode Island Rifleman.

55   A. Dilley: Off for a Stroll.

56   P. Wilcox: Roman Trooper
and Gothic Tribesman.

57 P. Wilcox: ... torian Tribune ... Standard-bearer.

58 P. Wilcox: Praetorian and Auxilia Roman Cavalry.

59 P. Wilcox: M... Trooper 13th Ce... A.D.

60   P. Wilcox: Roman Trooper and Marcomannic Prisoners.

61   P. Wilcox: Samnites 5th Century B.C.

62   P. Wilcox: Gothic Standard-bearer.

63   F. Verlinden: 6 pr. Anti-tank gun Portee.

64   N. Abbey: Return from Gettysburg.

65   R. Curty: Natal Mounted Police 1898.

66 P. Davies:
Lancers 1854.

67 D. Skinn
sian Anti-tank

68 D. Skinner: German Anti-tank Gun.

69 S. Ellis: 95th Rifleman in the Peninsular Campaign.

70 E. Pollard:
Grenadier Music

71 S. Kemp: Incident
at Lucknow.

72 I. J. Craig: Israeli Super-Sherman Tank.

73 J. Willis: 2nd Leib Garde and Potsdam Grenadier.

74 R. Pettit: Tamerlane.

75 A. T. Kettle: A Boer Amazon.

A BOER AMAZON
ELANDSLAAGTE

MC
33

76 G. Brown: Mokarex Historical Figure.

. Brown: Rich-
nd Officer.

78   G. Brown: French Voltigeur.

79   Sid Horton: German S.S. Cavalryman.

80 Sid Horton: Dismounted Figures from Balaklava.

Sid Horton: Groups
Balaklava.

82 J. Sandars: Marmon-Herrington Armoured Car.

83 W. Hearne: F
Garry Horse 1917.

84 W. Hearne: Arab
Legion Camel Trooper.

85 W. Hearne: (
man Motor-cycle
Crew.

86 W. Hearne: British 5th Lancers Bugler 1899–1902.

87 R. Dilley: Rolls-Royce Armoured Car.

88   J. Cuiffo: Casu
Clearing Station 19

89   D. Catley: Chey-
enne Indians with Cap-
tive.

90   R. Hapgood:
Marines Aircraft
rama.

91   A. T. Kettle: The Survivors 1812.

92   D. Catley: Indians Hunting.

93 D. Catley: quistadores.

94 C. Milani: Napoleon at Ravoli.

95 A. Dilley: Well at Cawnpore

96 A. Dilley: British
23rd Foot at Waterloo.

97 R. Dilley: A.T.S.
and Staff Car Group.

98 N. Infield: Napo-
leonic Soldiers Fishing.

99 R. Jeffries: Sherman Tank Diorama.

100 F. Verlinden: Anti-tank Gun in Action.

101 R. Skedgel: Mounted Indian in the Snow

R. Skedgel: Scout/
er.

103 M. Thomas: Officers and Colour, Royal Fusiliers.

B.Owen: W.A.A.C.
tch Rider.

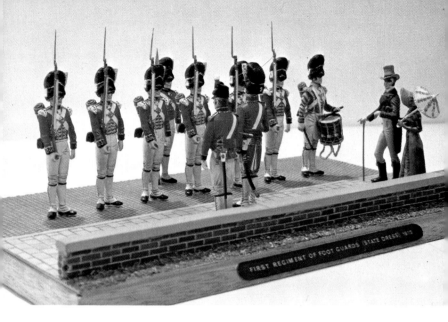

105 M. Tadman: 1st Foot Guards in Review 1815.

106 E. P. Staines: British Land Girl 1945.

107 C. Milani: Waterloo – the End.

A. T. Kettle: Ele-
... Battery in
...sinia.

109 D. Skinner: German Panzer IV Tank.

110 F. Verlinden: Grant Tank in the Desert.

111 D. Davis: 15th Hussars in Undress.

XVᵀᴴ HUSSARS 1822
(UNDRESS)

112   E. Leliepvre: Action at the Texel.

113   D. Disley: Royal Horse
Artillery Officer 1807.

114   M. Baldet: Poilu 1914-18.

115　K. Engledow: The Queen's
Own Hussars.

116　E. Leliepvre: Mounted Figure with Accoutrements.

117   E. Leliepvre: French Drummers.

118   J. Desfontaines: Street Scene in 18th Century Venice.

119   J. Desfontaines: War Elephant.

120   J. Desfontaines: Mediaeval Knights.

121 R. Lamb: Chasseur of the Guard.

122 R. Lamb: Carabiniers.

123   S. Paine: Elite Gendarmes.

124   S. Paine: Royal Scots Greys 1815.

125 P. Conrad: Lady Godiva Returns to the Convent.

126 P. Conrad: Napoleonic Horse Grenadier.

127   P. Conrad: Murat and Aide.

128   C. Stadden: Death of Nelson.

129　Leliepvre and Gilet: Napoleon Reviews his Troops.

130　P. Stearns: Roman Slave Market.

131   N. Abbey: Press-gang Raiding a Tavern.

132   N. Abbey: A 17th Century Inn.

133   R. Anderson: Consecration of John of Gaunt.

134   F. Verlinden:
U.S. Armoured
Personnel Carrier
in Vietnam.

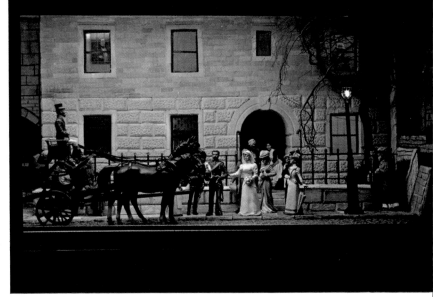

135 P. Stearns: A Victorian Military Wedding.

136 P. Stearns: Roman Slave Market (detail).

137   R. Dilley: Screw-gun in Action.

138   E. Suren: Majuba Hill 1881.

139   E. Suren: The Greys at Waterloo.

140   E. Suren: Aliwal (Sikh Wars).

Descriptions of the Colour Plates

Plate 1 – Early Britain's Cavalry. 1/32nd

It can truly be said that the introduction of hollow-cast metal figures by William Britain in the early 1890s paved the way for the astonishing success that the toy soldier was to enjoy as a cheap plaything for the next seventy years or so. Such pieces today command astronomical prices from collectors, and they can still be found in their original paint and sometimes even in their original boxes. These Britain's figures of British cavalry show how basically accurate this firm's products were in terms of anatomy and uniform detail. The figure second from the right represents a trooper of the Life Guards at the time of Waterloo, but in fact only the head and helmet are departures from the 1893 (contemporary) model.

John Ruddle Collection

Plate 2 – Britain's C.I.V. Ambulance Waggon. 1/32nd

Britain's included guns and gun-teams in their ranges from quite early on in their production, and later added ambulances and transport waggons. The piece illustrated is another rare item, from the period of the South African (Boer) War of 1899–1902, and was included in a set representative of the City Imperial Volunteers, a force drawn from London 'amateur' soldiers who went out to assist

125

the regular troops at the front. This example is in excellent condition, the original paint being scarcely damaged, and is in every respect typical of the care and attention to detail that went into Britain's products though they were, after all, intended only as children's toys. A C.I.V. infantryman is seen marching alongside the pairs of horses.

John Ruddle Collection

Plate 3 – Heyde Ambulance Waggon. 1/40th

Here, as an interesting contrast to Plate 2, is the Heyde version of an ambulance waggon. The vehicle is made from tin-plate, but has cast metal wheels and a real fabric hood or tilt, upon which is displayed a miniature Union Jack! All the nurses, medical personnel, horses and riders are cast in the standard way, that is solid metal. Heyde introduced enormous variety into their ranges of figures in all scales, to the extent in some cases of having removable helmets and equipment – and even scabbards from which the miniature swords could actually be withdrawn. The main disadvantage of these German figures as a whole was their comparatively high cost, which in effect confined their purchase and enjoyment to the middle and upper classes in whatever country they were sold.

John Ruddle Collection

Plate 4 – Mignot Types. 1/32nd

Fully modelled figures were produced in other countries than Germany and latterly Great Britain. Even before the end of the eighteenth century this type of model was being manufactured in France and continued to appear thereafter. Perhaps the most prominent firms were Lucotte, C.B.G. and Mignot; the latter absorbed the other two companies but still continued to turn out models from their moulds as well as true Mignot pieces. Mignot have carried on production of solid metal figures to this day. The plate shows some of their attractive figures, which also spanned a very

126

considerable historical period and encompassed an enormous range of types.

John Ruddle Collection

Plate 5 – Modern Toy Figures. 54mm

It would be more accurate to refer to these pieces as being in the tradition of toy soldiers, since their cost and the material from which they are cast would seem to bar them as playthings from all but the very well-to-do in those areas of the world which have not outlawed the use of lead and lead alloys in the production of toys. These Indian Army Mountain Artillerymen with their mules and screw-gun split down into its various parts have been designed by Barry Minot and are part of a range of pieces depicting the late Victorian period.

Courtesy of J. Coutts

Plate 6 – Modern Toy Figures. 54mm

This is another view of the Indian Army figures shown in Plate 5, and serves to illustrate the realistic and attractive nature of many mass-produced figures now available to collectors.

Courtesy of J. Coutts

Plate 7 – Paper Cut-outs. 1/12th

Subjects, both military and civilian, printed on stout paper sheets and intended to be cut out into individual pieces, often with some kind of in-built method of enabling them to stand up, were for many years produced as an attempt to get round the high cost of metal figures, as well as providing charming miniatures in their own right. This modern sheet, by the Wolfe Publishing Company, is of the dress-up type in which items of dress, equipment and armament are designed to be fitted on to a basically clad figure by means of slots and tabs.

Courtesy of Seagull Models

Plate 8 – Ammunition Mule and Handler. 54mm

This interesting little group shows an example of the type of back-up service that accompanied troops on campaign or during field-days at the end of the last century. Ample supplies of ammunition were essential to get the best effect from the recently introduced magazine-rifles and various kinds of machine-guns. Pack animals, such as the mule, were frequently employed to ensure that reserve ammunition was immediately available to troops in action.

Courtesy of J. Coutts

Plate 9 – Rose Models: Cretan Bull Group. 54mm
Among the leading manufacturers of connoisseur models for many years, Russell Gammage – under his trade-mark Rose Models – has established a world-wide reputation for work of a consistently high standard. Specialities in his extensive catalogue covering many periods are ranges of figures representing types from the ancient world. This unusual group, including a princess and priestess, as well as the acrobats and bull in full career, is typical of the ancients to be found in Russell's comprehensive output.

Gammage Collection

Plate 10 – Wolfe Publishing: Paper Figures. 1/12th
The attractive results of cutting out and dressing the kind of figure shown in Plate 7 is illustrated by these elegant hussars of the Napoleonic period. They are about eight inches in height and, as the plate shows, allow a very considerable amount of detail to be incorporated.

Courtesy of Seagull Models

Plate 11 – Ensign Miniatures: British Mess-kit 1900. 54mm
Modern production techniques have enabled distinguished sculptors and designers to provide figures of the very highest standard for the present-day collector and hobbyist. Among the finest examples of these so-called connoisseur pieces are Major Bob Rowe's beautifully posed figures showing British Army Officers

128

of the 1900 period in their formal evening wear, known as 'mess-kit'.

Rowe Collection

Plate 12 – Ensign Miniatures: Highlanders. 54mm

Another of Bob Rowe's delightful vignettes, depicting Scottish soldiers. A private of the Black Watch leans cross-legged against a tree stump, chatting with his comrade from the Gordon Highlanders. Although only a few inches square the scenic base provides a convincing location for these solid metal pre-animated figures.

Rowe Collection

Plate 13 – Rose Models: Egyptian Chariot. 54mm

Full of movement and vitality, this superb vehicle group is justly popular among enthusiasts for figures from ancient history. The piece has been painted with great skill, and achieves added realism from its careful placing in an authentic environment.

Gammage Collection

Plate 14 – Charles Stadden: Redcoat and Redskin. 54mm

There is no doubt that the master sculptor Charles Stadden, with his monumental ranges of figures covering almost every period, played a part in the establishment and enormous expansion of interest in military miniatures that has taken place over the last quarter of a century. Stadden's work finds an honoured place in serious collections all over the world, and his standards of accuracy and craftsmanship are of the very highest. This pair has been photographed against a 'natural' background by means of a technique developed by Philip Stearns himself.

Philip O. Stearns Collection

Plate 15 – Charles Stadden: Corner of a British Square at Waterloo. 54mm

In this large group, which has maximum impact on the observer, the British Infantry figures have been animated after casting to give a variety of attitudes to what is essentially a single basic casting. Much of Stadden's earlier work was carried out in this way, but in recent years he has made much more use of techniques in which the figures are cast in their finished poses.

Courtesy of Tradition

Plate 16 – Charles Stadden: Burning the Colours. 54mm
Involving a large number of figures in many attitudes with horses and equipment, this large scenic setting or diorama, as the style has come to be termed among modellers, conveys much of the poignancy and desolation surrounding this incident, which occurred during the disastrous French Retreat from Moscow in the year 1812.

Courtesy of Tradition

Plate 17 – Flight Deck of a Space-ship. 54mm
This boxed or cased diorama is one of several featured in this colour section (the others appear together, from Plate 128 onwards). In this type of diorama the subject, often with integral lighting, is presented to be viewed from one side, i.e. the 'open', glazed front of the case. Such an arrangement permits effects, notably of perspective, that would not be possible in an uncased diorama or scenic setting (which could, of course, be viewed from any direction). This imaginative scene, depicting a science-fiction subject, has been most ingeniously composed and lit by a competitor in a recent Historex Competition, the figures in the composition being conversions of components manufactured by that company.

Courtesy of Historex

Plate 18 – Series 77: Weapons Collection. 150mm
This impressive display of arms and armour, set against dark wood panelling, could easily be taken for the real thing. Each piece has been meticulously modelled on its prototype, polished, painted, and placed in position on its display base. These pieces, cast in white

130

metal, are among the finest miniatures of weaponry available to collectors.

Bird Collection

Plate 19 – Series 77: English Civil War Group. 77mm

More larger scale models, demonstrating the realism and attention to detail achieved by Pat Bird's artistry. Here the varying contours of the scenic base allow the figures to be set at different levels, and this gives additional variety and interest to the presentation of the piece.

Bird Collection

Plate 20 – Series 77: Ancient Greeks. 77mm

Textures of flesh, metal, cloth, hide and stone have been interestingly combined in this group of 'ancients'. The horse is particularly well modelled, and the musician with his lyre adds an unusual touch.

Bird Collection

Plate 21 – Greenwood and Ball: The Sudan 1898. 54mm

Set in the time of the Anglo-Egyptian re-conquest of the Sudan in 1898, this scene depicts British soldier prisoners in the hands of the Dervish forces. All the figures of the natives are designed by John Tassel, and the British are 'Olive' figures somewhat converted. The background is largely made up from expanded polystyrene, with some cast-metal Britain's palm trees to provide colour and sense of location. Greenwood and Ball manufacture their products from 'masters' designed by many of the leading miniaturists of today.

Assembled, painted and owned by George Hanger

Plate 22 – Imrie/Risley: World War II German Paratroops. 54mm

The work of the celebrated U.S. designer Bill Imrie, these German paratroopers have been photographed using Philip Stearns' 'natural' technique, which has succeeded particularly well in this shot. Standard figures, cast in white metal, from the Imrie/Risley range have been utilized, nicely painted, and posed most effectively against a 'real' background.

Imrie/Risley Collection

Plate 23 – Imrie/Risley: U.S. Cavalry in the South-west. 30mm

Just how striking smaller scales can be is very apparent in this diorama by Bill Imrie, which again makes use of 30mm figures. Set in the arid desert areas of the American South-west during the Indian Wars of the 1880s, it conveys very faithfully the difficult and challenging nature of the terrain in which the U.S. Army of the period had to seek its elusive foes.

Imrie/Risley Collection

Plate 24 – John Tassel: North British Dragoon 1752. 130mm

Beautifully painted and photographed against a pleasant background this large-scale figurine is an excellent example of the sculpture of another former colleague of Chas. Stadden, John Tassel, who is known among collectors for his brilliant Lasset ranges of figures encompassing a great many periods from ancient times to World War II. John's work is very distinctive and the majority of his figures are animated after casting. This dragoon is typical of the style and competence of a designer of the highest quality.

Philip O. Stearns Collection

Plate 25 – Phoenix Models: U.S. Marines. 75mm

This pair of figures, in one of the larger scales, depicts men of this famous corps in the uniform worn at the time of its formation, and at the present day. A rising star in the field of miniature sculpture, Tim Richards, was responsible for the design of these figures, which reveal an excellent appreciation of the requirements of anatomy, drapery and uniform detail. Beautifully cast in solid

132

white metal, these are top-quality examples of commercially produced models.

Philip O. Stearns Collection

Plate 26 – Realmodels: Scout. 90mm

Representative of the same period as Plate 23, but in a much larger scale and designed by Bill Hearne, is this Army Scout. These scouts were more often than not civilians employed on a temporary basis by the military. Many of them spent practically their whole adult lives in contact with Indians, and they provided the soldiers with information and guidance in their constant efforts to contain the tribes.

A. Campbell Collection

Plate 27 – Strolling in the Park. 54mm

The work of a prominent English modeller, Sid Horton, this group has added interest in that it includes figures from several designers, which Sid has painted and placed in a scenic setting to make a harmonious whole. On the left of the piece the soldier walking with his lady friend is from a Cliff Sanderson master figure, as are the lady with the little girl in the centre of the group and the elegant lady carrying the umbrella on the right. Placed by the latter is the figure of a more middle-aged lady, a creation by Roger Saunders (another young sculptor whose work is earning wide acclaim), while the central piece – an elderly man – is the work of Alan Caton, well known for his association with Tradition and latterly his own company All the Queen's Men. It will be seen that, despite the variety of their origins, these same-scale models fit quite happily together in this elegant little Horton group.

A. Campbell Collection

Plate 28 – Imrie/Risley: Chasseur of the Garde. 54mm

With this plate we return to the work of Bill Imrie, one of whose characteristics is his masterly interpretation of horses, their anatomy and conformations when in motion. The elegance of the

133

animal shown in this example is an indication of Bill's competence, and the easy attitude of its rider is also a delight to behold.

Imrie/Risley Collection

Plate 29 – New Hope Design: Landsknechts, early Sixteenth Century. 54mm

These are some of the large number of models created for New Hope Design by the sculptor Malcolm Dawson. The figures are cast in white metal and are produced individually; they go together, however, into an attractive group, and include a sutleress with her donkey laden with supplies. As with most connoisseur pieces, the amount of applied and engraved detail requires patience and skill in painting; but given this, and some imagination in setting them into an environment, they become very rewarding show pieces.

Philip O. Stearns Collection

Plate 30 – Rose Models: Napoleonic Infantry in Egypt. 54mm

Based on French troops involved in the Egyptian Campaign of 1798–1801, these infantrymen are typical of the high quality achieved by many of today's master modellers in producing figures commercially. They are cast in solid white metal, but arms, weapons and accessories are made as separate items to be fixed on by the collector himself before painting. This system, in addition to allowing for more animation in the basic figure and minimizing difficult under-cuts in the moulds, also permits a certain scope for the collector to produce a final result with something of his own imaginative ability involved.

Gammage Collection

Plate 31 – Rose Models: Persian Immortals. 54mm

In this colourful group are depicted more of the 'ancient' subjects interpreted so well by Rose designers. The attraction of the ancient world is becoming more widespread among collectors generally, and much more supportive data in the form of books, illustrations, discourses on military life and tactics of those far-off times is becoming available. Models such as those shown here would surely find a prominent place in the collection of any modeller seriously interested in early and exotic subjects.

Gammage Collection

Plate 32 – Greenwood and Ball: Types of the U.S. Indian Wars. 54mm

Among the multitude of pieces produced by this manufacturer from the 'masters' of a number of designers are to be found a small but increasing range of unusual subjects created by Al Charles. His work is full of character, even caricature in some instances, but it generally deals with areas not commonly covered to any great extent by the products of other manufacturers. The plate illustrates Al's characteristic style.

Courtesy of Greenwood and Ball

Plate 33 – Airfix Products: Scene in Western Desert 1942. 54mm

One of the most significant factors in the development of the military miniature hobby over the last decade or so has been the increasing use by manufacturers of one or other of the plastic materials in the production of cheap yet highly detailed models. In this diorama made up from assembly kits by François Verlinden, a celebrated Belgian modeller, figures, vehicle, weapons and palm trees are all plastic; yet properly assembled, finished and painted, they are indistinguishable from the best metal models.

Verlinden Collection

Plate 34 – Airfix Products: 'Who? Me?' 1943. 54mm

The flexibility afforded to modellers – in terms of figure attitudes and armaments – by the 'Multipose' system adopted by Airfix Products for a complete range of World War II soldier sets in 54mm scale, means that even newcomers to the hobby can arrive at unusual and even unique items just by swopping around the parts, all of which are designed (in the same precise scale) to be completely interchangeable. The 'master' figures for this range have been created by Ronald Cameron, a sculptor and artist of international reputation. This small diorama of a British 8th Army soldier confronted by a corporal of Military Police was put together by the author entirely from Multipose parts, with a modicum of sand, rock and dried moss to form the desert background.

Airfix Collection

Plate 35 – Airfix Products: Afrika Korps 1943. 54mm

Another example of the Multipose system utilized by the author with two members of the much-vaunted Afrika Korps set in a desert environment. Each of the Multipose World War II sets, of which there are seven, comprises about one hundred parts and is intended to make up into six figures. The opportunities for variation are therefore almost unlimited, not to mention the veritable bonanza that the series offers to converters and scratch-builders.

Airfix Collection

Plate 36 – Hinchliffe Models: Gatling-gun and Detachment. 54mm

During the 1860s the British Service authorities decided to take a detailed look at mechanically operated repeating guns, and weapons were purchased from a number of inventors, several of them from the U.S.A., and subjected to evaluation procedures. This prize-winning diorama by the author depicts the scene at Shoeburyness in 1867, when the 1in.-calibre Gatling-gun was being put through its paces. The model weapon is from the excellent range of cast-metal miniature pieces of artillery that is produced in kit form by Hinchliffe Models, and is served by a detachment of model Victorian gunners, from the same manufacturer, subjected to only minimal animation and conversion. Thick cardboard and various items of railway scenic accessories, grass matting, painted and embossed card, etc., were used in the construction of the gun-embrasure setting.

Dilley Collection

Plate 37 – Squadron/Rubin: Moonmaid. 54mm

Fantasy subjects are enjoying a considerable vogue among miniaturists at the present time, and several sculptors of renown have produced items showing great ability – and vigorous use of the imagination. Such a piece, by American Ray Rubin, cast in white metal, contrasts the comely, sparsely clad female with her ferocious centaur-like mount. The piece has been painted and photographed against a real-life shot of the Earth, taken during one of the moon landings.

Philip O. Stearns Collection

Plate 38 – Historex: Napoleonic 4th Cuirassier. 54mm

Among the model-making manufacturers who adopted plastics as the medium for their products, and helped to make it respectable among enthusiasts by the sheer quality of their designs, one of the undoubted leaders is the French company of Historex. Their assembly kits, overwhelmingly of Napoleonic subjects, are moulded in rigid polystyrene plastic and can be put together with flair and careful techniques to produce truly exquisite representations of their real-life prototypes. One of the finest exponents of the art of plastic-figure assembly, conversion and painting is Graham Brown of London, whose figure of a cuirassier, bending forward in the saddle to pluck a lady's handkerchief from a clump of gorse with his sword point, demonstrates the high standards that can be achieved with this type of kit.

G. Brown Collection

Plate 39 – Historex: Napoleonic Lancer. 54mm

Some of the most effective Historex assembly conversion and dioramic presentations have been carried out by Max Longhurst, a Londoner whose reputation has been established over the years by consistent successes in competition with the finest modellers in Europe and the United Kingdom. Max is perhaps at his best with mounted subjects, and this example of his work shows the meticulous care with which he renders every detail of rider and mount, with particular attention to the textures concerned. Together with

Graham Brown, mentioned in connection with Plate 38, Max is most proficient at passing on his skills and techniques to others, and gives regular demonstrations of modelling practices at important meetings and displays in England, Belgium and France.

Longhurst Collection

Plate 40 – Phoenix Models: Atlantis Fantasy Scene. 54mm

In this fantasy group from Phoenix miniatures the outstanding ability of designer Tim Richards in the representation of anatomy and drapery is well demonstrated. The ladies may be a little over-endowed in certain respects, but this is allowable – even expected – in fantasy figures, and all the work is of a most laudable nature. The conformation and ferocious aspect of the chained leopard can scarcely have been surpassed by any sculptor of miniatures. Tim Richards also painted these pieces, which are part of a continuing range with the Atlantean theme, and they have been photographed against a suitable unusual background.

Richards Collection

Plate 41 – Zinnfiguren – Ancient Types. 40mm

Tin soldiers are among the earliest and most traditional of mass-produced toy figures, although in truth their composition – as the original metal became more expensive – was likely to be pewter, or alloys of tin, lead, antimony and even a little copper. In addition to being cheaper than pure tin, the later alloys proved to be more robust. Produced as flat two–dimensional pieces, *Zinnfiguren* were often remarkable for the artistic merit of the engraving, and provided ideal surfaces upon which painters could practise their skills. One of the foremost exponents of the art of painting flats today is Jim Woodley, examples of whose exquisite work are shown in the plate. Flats are often thought of as being best suited for mass effects, but close examination of Woodley's work will reveal that each is a little masterpiece in its own right.

Woodley Collection

138

Plate 42 – Zinnfiguren – Various Types. 30mm
These further examples of Jim Woodley's work with flats emphasize the grace and vitality that can be conveyed by really skilful painting of two-dimensional subjects. Over the two centuries or more that *Zinnfiguren* have been produced, a truly vast variety of subjects has appeared, covering virtually every aspect of human life from the earliest times to the present day. Flats are especially popular among Continental collectors, particularly in Germany (where most manufacturing still takes place).

Woodley Collection

Plate 43 – Zinnfiguren – Hussar. 30mm
Although not as widespread as on the Continent, flats do have their devotees in Britain and the U.S.A. This example of a hussar of Frederick the Great's time has been beautifully painted by Richard K. Riehn, a noted American collector and painter whose work rivals that of any enthusiast for flats, wherever he may be found. The treatment of drapery – the soldier's cloak – is particularly well done in this piece.

Riehn Collection

Plate 44 – Zinnfiguren – Potsdam Parade. 30mm
Here we see flats in a massed effect, representing a ceremonial parade with Frederick the Great and his 'Giant Grenadiers' at Potsdam. The detail on all the figures has been picked out with skill, and the whole effect is evocative of the period.

Riehn Collection

Plate 45 – Zinnfiguren – Staff Conference. 30mm
Not only human and animal figures are produced in the vast ranges of flats, but scenic features, vehicles, furniture, architecture, and indeed almost everything with shape and substance has, at one time or another, been represented, and examples can be seen among the selection of pieces illustrated in this book. This plate shows how the

use of trees heightens the sombre effect of the Frederickan staff conference taking place below them.

Riehn Collection

Plate 46 – Zinnfiguren – Mounted Officer. 30mm

One of the most attractive attributes to be found among the great engravers of flats is the fidelity with which animals are portrayed in form and motion. In this example the balance and conformation of the animal are conveyed exactly, and, although not in violent movement, its nervous energy comes through very strongly as a result of the designer's skill.

Riehn Collection

Plate 47 – Zinnfiguren – Plains Indians. 30mm

These splendid mounted Redskins typify the vitality and diversity of subject material so characteristic of *Zinnfiguren*. Whatever an enthusiast's specialized interest may be, the likelihood is that miniatures related to it will be found among the products of the manufacturers of flats.

McGerr Collection

Plate 48 – Zinnfiguren – Exotic Animals. 30mm

In this set an Egyptian Pharaoh is receiving homage and gifts. It is remarkable for the representations of animals, the designer's work heightened by the superlative painting skills of Jim Woodley. The gorgeous giraffe dominates this set, towering above even the Pharaoh's covered throne.

Woodley Collection

Plate 49 – Zinnfiguren – Roman Feast. 30mm

How thoroughly and with what gusto did the wealthy Romans indulge their various appetites! Here patricians are being entertained, literally, with wine, women and song. Dancers, musicians and plentiful supplies of wine contribute to an evening to remember!

Woodley Collection

Plate 50 – Zinnfiguren – Egyptian Court Scenes. 30mm

Even though much the same ingredients are involved – food, drink, dancing and music – these Egyptians of rank seem to be taking their pleasures in a much more serious and decorous manner than the Romans in the previous plate. Jim Woodley has been particularly successful in his rendering of the diaphanous draperies worn by some of the figures in this scene.

Woodley Collection

Plate 51 – D. Catley: Moghul Procession. 54mm

With this plate we commence a section devoted to the work of exponents of the arts of conversion and scratch-building (both terms explained elsewhere in the text). David Catley built this diorama of a bygone age in India, using Historex components and scrap plastic, paper, wood and plaster. Since Historex designs are almost exclusively of Napoleonic subjects, some idea of the adaptation and re-working that was necessary can be obtained by close study of this fascinating piece.

Philip O. Stearns Collection

Plate 52 – R. Dilley: M5 Half-track. 54mm

This illustration of a World War II diorama by the author shows the effect of detailing and/or conversion applied to a basic commercial assembly kit. The vehicle, weapons, some paraphernalia and soldiers are made of plastic, with other materials – metal, paper, wood and cloth – introduced during the conversion processes. Displayed on a polished wooden base with a scenically textured surface the model is representative of the type of vehicle used by the Allies in North-western Europe during 1944–45.

Dilley Collection

Plate 53 – R. Dilley: 'Near Kalemyo' 1944. 54mm

Another example by the author of converted plastic assembly kits of vehicle and figures placed in a scenic environment. Representative of the World War II campaign in Burma, it depicts a military police staging post on the lines of communication on the Central Front. The signpost represented really existed!

Dilley Collection

Plate 54 – Jeff Burns: Rhode Island Rifleman 1776. 150mm

A large-scale figurine made in wood and plaster and dressed in garments of real leather and cloth, this is a beautiful example of the modeller's art by Jeff Burns. The figure is attractively posed and perfectly balanced, and the long rifle with which it is armed is a miniature masterpiece in itself.

Philip O. Stearns Collection

Plate 55 – Anthony Dilley: 'Off for a Stroll' 1942. 54mm

A conversion of Airfix Multipose items with a scratch-built scout car in the background, this soldier of the 8th Army in North Africa is taking his spade for a walk – a euphemism that will be understood by most persons with any experience of service life! The work of the author's son, this piece demonstrates how well the Multipose system responds to careful assembly and painting, and a touch of imagination.

Dilley Collection

Plate 56 – Peter Wilcox: Roman Heavy Trooper. 54mm

A producer of truly original work, scratch-building his models with whatever materials seem to be most suitable for a particular subject, Peter Wilcox is one of the best known and consistent members of the modelling fraternity. Specializing in subjects from the ancient world and dark ages, Peter is also a respected researcher of these eras, and builds his considerable knowledge of and feeling for the times into his models. This third-century A.D. Roman cavalryman looks down dispassionately at the snow-covered corpse of a Gothic tribesman.

Wilcox Collection

Plate 57 – Peter Wilcox: Praetorian Tribune and Standard-bearer. 54mm

These, too, are the result of painstaking research, and reflect much of the dignity, splendour and not inconsiderable technology of the Roman Empire. Even the painting on the standard is done in an authentic Roman style. The officer stands on real marble steps.

Wilcox Collection

Plate 58 – Peter Wilcox: Praetorian and Auxilia Cavalry. 54mm

Representing 'Guard' and 'line' cavalry, these pieces show the combined effect of research, modelling skills and applied imagination. Peter is particularly adept in the simulation of metallic surfaces of all kinds.

Wilcox Collection

Plate 59 – Peter Wilcox: Mongol Trooper. 54mm

In this piece Peter has produced a striking representation of the type of Mongol horseman who swept in hordes across Asia and Eastern Europe during the early mediaeval period. Subject, modelling, painting and presentation are all indicative of the high standards incorporated into every Wilcox item.

Wilcox Collection

Plate 60 – Peter Wilcox: Roman Trooper and Marcomannic Prisoners. 54mm

Very few nations or tribes found it very profitable to take on the Romans at the height of their power! In this little vignette can be seen the almost inevitable result.

Wilcox Collection

Plate 61 – Peter Wilcox: Samnites 5th Century B.C. 54mm

More 'ancients', showing the meticulous care and attention with which subject and setting, however simple, are handled in Peter's presentations.

Wilcox Collection

143

Plate 62 – Peter Wilcox: Gothic Standard-bearer. 54mm

This is a superb mounted figure, horse and rider blending in a presentation of great power and impact. It is with pieces of this quality that the claim of the military miniaturist that his work is a true art-form can be fully substantiated.

Wilcox Collection

Plate 63 – François Verlinden: 6 pr Portee. 54mm

An expert Belgian modeller, specializing in the meticulous assembly of plastic kits and their presentation in scenic environments, Verlinden has here developed a World War II subject with a lorry-mounted anti-tank gun and two British soldiers in the Western Desert, for whom the Airfix Multipose system provided the basic parts.

Verlinden Collection

Plate 64 – Norman Abbey: Return from Gettysburg.54mm

American Civil War subjects are popular throughout the modelling world, not merely with modellers in North America. In this vignette Norman Abbey, with figures converted from Historex items, has re-created some of the poignancy and dejection felt by the Southern forces after the Battle of Gettysburg.

Abbey Collection

Plate 65 – Rene Curty: Natal Mounted Police. 54mm

Southern Africa in the closing years of the last century is the scene for this spirited little representation of a police patrol operating in wild country. An officer and three constables are depicted, and Rene Curty has done a remarkable job in reproducing the uniform and weaponry detail so accurately.

Curty Collection

Plate 66 – Peter Davies: 17th Lancers 1854. 150mm

Airfix's large-scale plastic show jumper assembly kit provided the basis for this excellent representation of a trooper of the 17th Lancers in the uniform worn at the Charge of the Light Brigade at Balaklava, 1854. The trooper is in campaign uniform, with the

144

foul-weather cover over his 'schapska' cap, and the pennon of his lance furled and secured. In the foreground can be seen part of a companion figure in the presentation, an officer of the 11th Hussars.

Davies Collection

Plate 67 – Donald Skinner: Russian 76mm Anti-tank Gun. 1/35th

Another manufacturer's example, made simply but definitely characteristic of World War II locations. The short curving lengths of tram-lines suggest an urban environment with a minimum of effort.

Kohnstam Collection

Plate 68 – Donald Skinner: German Anti-tank Gun. 1/35th

Part of a series of dioramas created by a professional model maker for promotional purposes by the kit-manufacturers, this pleasing little vignette points out the added impact given to a figure or group by placing in even a simple environment. The gun and its detachment are assembled straight from the kit, but skilfully painted and placed into position in the setting by Donald Skinner they make an extremely effective presentation.

Kohnstam Collection

Plate 69 – S. Ellis: Sergeant 95th Rifles 1808–9. 75mm

This excellently painted and presented large-scale piece was a prize-winner in an important international competition. Considerable skill and imagination have been shown in mounting what is basically a proprietary Hinchliffe Models figure into an imaginative environment suggesting the rigours of the Peninsular Campaign.

Ellis Collection

Plate 70 – E. Pollard: Musician of Dutch Grenadiers 1810. 54mm

Negroes were commonly employed by many nations as musicians, usually percussionists, in the military bands of the period. Ed.

145

Pollard's Historex conversion has life and character, is made more effective by the use of a few accessories – the dog, barrel, unusual 'Jingling Johnnie' instrument, etc. – and is placed in a neat environment, attractively mounted.

Pollard Collection

Plate 71 – S. Kemp: Incident at Lucknow 1858. 54mm

Depicting an incident in the Great Mutiny of 1857–58, this prize-winning group was converted from a mixture of basic items from Airfix and Historex plastic ranges. Brushed nylon hair has been used for the horses' manes and tails and a really impressive sense of movement and impact has been achieved.

Kemp Collection

Plate 72 – I. J. Craig: Israeli Super-Sherman. 54mm

This interpretation of an incident in the Yom Kippur War won a Silver Medal for the modeller at a recent exhibition in London. Both vehicle and personnel are plastic pieces, conversions of commercial assembly kits, beautifully assembled and painted. The representation of the anti-tank gun emplacement and desert terrain is also extremely well done.

Craig Collection

Plate 73 – J. Willis: 2nd Leib Garde and Potsdam Grenadier 1750. 77mm

These Prussian soldiers of the time of Frederick the Great are really excellent examples of beautifully painted larger-scale figures. The groundwork has been kept deliberately simple, but the polished wood bases enhance the fine quality of these attractively finished pieces.

Philip O. Stearns Collection

Plate 74 – R. Pettit: Tamerlane. 54mm

Converted from an Airfix collectors' series plastic assembly kit, this figure reveals a very great deal of imaginative application of data and techniques. The armour and horse furniture are particu-

146

larly well constructed, and considerable skill is apparent in the painting of a difficult subject.

Pettit Collection

Plate 75 – A. T. Kettle: A Boer Amazon. 54mm

A prize-winning piece from a gifted amateur with a consistently high-quality output of figures, this model depicts one of the Boer ladies who joined their men 'on Kommando' during the South African War, 1899–1902. Incorporating metal and plastic components in their construction, the figures are nicely presented in an environment reminiscent of the rocky 'kloofs' and 'kopjes' over which much of the action in that war took place.

Kettle Collection

Plate 76 – Graham Brown: Mokarex figure. 60mm

This plastic figure, one of several series originally designed as give-away items for the coffee company Mokarex, has been prepared, painted and placed in a presentation setting by one of the finest of the young British modellers. The painting, carried out in artists' oil colours, is superlatively well done, and turns a free-gift item, albeit of excellent basic design, into what can be described as a miniature masterpiece.

G. Brown Collection

Plate 77 – Graham Brown: Richlieu and Officer. 60mm

Further items from the Mokarex series, delightfully painted and presented. Many of the pieces from these series can now be purchased independently of the original coffee product, and those new to the hobby could do a lot worse than use these economically priced figures in the development of their own painting techniques.

G. Brown Collection

Plate 78 – Graham Brown: Napoleonic Voltigeur. 54mm

In this piece Graham Brown demonstrates all his skills of animation, painting and imaginative presentation. Made of plastic Historex and Airfix components, the figure is exquisitely assembled and painted, while the groundwork and balance of the piece fully justify its prize-winning status.

G. Brown Collection

Plate 79 – Sid Horton: S. S. Cavalryman 1942. 54mm

Designer Sid Horton is particularly well known among military modellers for his imaginative conversions, especially of horses, using Historex and Airfix plastic components as his basic material. In this example of his work an Airfix Napoleonic Hussar has been transformed into a German Cavalryman of World War II.

Horton Collection

Plate 80 – Sid Horton: 'Return from Balaklava' figures. 54mm

Working towards the reconstruction in dioramic form of the famous canvas by Lady Butler entitled 'Balaklava, Return from the Charge', Sid Horton has produced a number of subjects from the painting which are illustrated in the plate. All are conversions of plastic items, mostly Airfix, and demonstrate the skill and ingenuity of this enthusiast's work.

Horton Collection

Plate 81 – Sid Horton: Groups from Balaklava. 54mm

More sub-groups from the Balaklava diorama which indicate Sid's skills in conversion. The grey horse lying dead in the bottom right-hand corner of the illustration is a massive conversion of a plastic Airfix model in which the animal is displayed at full gallop!

Horton Collection

Plate 82 – John Sandars: Marmon-Herrington Armoured Car 1941. 54mm

The work of an enthusiast who has made a special study of all aspects of the campaigns in North Africa during World War II, this excellently modelled armoured car is typical of the equipment used by British reconnaissance units during the period 1941–42. John, a retired naval officer, makes many of his models using card rather than plastic sheet as his basic material, and is a recognized authority on Desert War vehicles as well as being a Vice President of the British Model Soldier Society.

Sandars Collection

Plate 83 – William Hearne: Fort Garry Horse 1917. 54mm

Among the best known modellers operating in the United Kingdom and North America, Bill Hearne – currently a professional designer of military miniatures – has the enviable ability to make almost every model he produces special in some way. There will usually be some item of detail or aspect of technique employed that will engage the attention and compel the admiration of modelling enthusiasts, whatever their degree of competitive or special interest. This splendid cavalryman, in all the paraphernalia of service in World War I, is typical of Bill's work.

Hearne Collection

Plate 84 – William Hearne: Camel Trooper. 54mm

Another example of the skill and attention to detail that go into Bill Hearne's creations. There are in excess of forty tassels in the camel's trappings, and the painting of man, animal and equipment is meticulous.

Hearne Collection

Plate 85 – William Hearne: German Motor-cycle and Crew 1942. 1/9th

For this large-scale presentation Bill specially created the two German figures to fit a commercially produced motor-cycle combination plastic assembly kit. The result of Bill's work in assembling and detailing the combination, crewing it with his unique figures and presenting it on a scenic base is an outstandingly realistic model.

Hearne Collection

Plate 86 – William Hearne: Bugler of the 5th Lancers 1899–1902. 54mm

Based on a well-known painting by R. Caton-Woodville, this superb cavalry figure won overall Champion of Show at an Annual Competition of the International Plastic Modellers' Society. Converted from Historex components, and assembled with all Bill's skill and experience, this truly represents the very highest standards of military modelling.

Hearne Collection

Plate 87 – Roy Dilley: Rolls Royce Armoured Car 1940. 54mm

Representative of the cars used by the British 11th Hussars during the early months of the World War II desert campaigns, this model is presented as if halted at the barbed wire of the Egyptian–Libyan frontier. This is a scratch-built model – plastic-sheet used as the basis for its construction – and only the wheels are commercially produced items.

Dilley Collection

Plate 88 – John Cuiffo: Casualty Clearing Station. 54mm

This brilliant modeller achieves the most life-like results using plasticene modelling clay as the base material for his figures. He also has an outstanding ability to create convincing scenic settings, and this sombre World War I subject reveals how effectively his techniques operate to convey the desired effects.

Cuiffo Collection

Plate 89 – David Catley: Cheyenne Indians with Captive. 54mm

With consummate skill the artist has achieved in this diorama a true sense of atmosphere of the Old West. Every detail and texture of cloth, hair and feathers has been faithfully rendered, and the terrain is suitably barren and dusty. Historex components in polystyrene plastics were used as the bases for these amazingly effective conversions.

Catley Collection

Plate 90 – Ray Hapgood: U.S. Marines Aircraft Diorama. 54mm

Full of bustle and urgency, this diorama of activity on board an aircraft carrier combines the modelling of men and machines in a most compelling way. In order to succeed with this type of presentation a modeller must be master of a whole range of techniques, and Ray Hapgood's abilities have made him a consistent prize-winner at exhibitions and competitions. This piece has been acquired by the U. S. Marines for display in their Corps museum.

U. S. Marines Museum

Plate 91 – A. T. Kettle: The Survivors 1812. 54mm

The retreat of the French Grand Army from Moscow in 1812 has provided inspiration for models of all kinds, from flat *Zinnfiguren* to large figurines. In this instance an accomplished modeller, working in standard 54mm scale, has produced a poignant little group which typifies the whole tragic affair (which resulted in the loss of virtually an entire army). Well thought out and presented, this vignette makes the point that Napoleon's soldiers were not always *point-de-vice* in brightly coloured uniforms smothered in cords and lace!

Kettle Collection

Plate 92 – David Catley: Indians Hunting. 54mm

In a snow-scene of great power, David Catley manages to convey the bitterly cold bleakness of winter in the American far north. Again Historex plastic figures have been converted to splendid effect, and the whole composition is a considerable artistic and technical achievement.

Catley Collection

Plate 93 – David Catley: Conquistadores. 54mm

Yet another of David Catley's artistic groups, these Historex and Airfix plastic conversions make an attractive composition utilizing one of the more unusual subjects for military figures.

Catley Collection

Plate 94 – Cesare Milani: Napoleon at Ravoli. 54mm

The work of a prominent Italian modeller, resident in London, this group based on a well-known painting consists of conversions of Historex plastic components. Nicely modelled, painted and presented, this is a good example of the effects achieved by an enthusiast who started off by modelling aeroplanes!

C. Milani Collection

Plate 95 – Anthony Dilley: The Well at Cawnpore 1857. 54mm

During the Indian Mutiny of 1857–58, more than two hundred European women and children were murdered in a particularly barbaric atrocity by the mutineers or their adherents, and the bodies were flung down a disused well shaft. The diorama shows the horrified reactions of the first British soldiers to discover the ghastly results of the massacre. Nicely understated, there is a minimum of blood and no 'horrors' at all in the piece; the composition allows the attitudes of the soldiers themselves to indicate their grief, revulsion and desire for revenge. Shown in its construction stages in a television programme dealing with military modelling, this prize-winning presentation deserves the wide acclaim it has received (and employed plastic conversions of Airfix, Historex and Almark figures).

Dilley Collection

Plate 96 – Anthony Dilley: 23rd Foot at Waterloo. 54mm

In contrast to the previous plate, this single-figure presentation is a straight assembly of a metal figure designed by Charles Stadden. Anthony's painting of the piece and its positioning on a small scenic base combine with Stadden's casting to result in an effective study of the type of infantryman who stood the test so well at Waterloo.

Dilley Collection

Plate 97 – Roy Dilley: A.T.S. and Staff Car 1944. 54mm

Not all soldiers, of course, are male. Since World War I, women have noticeably taken an increasing part in military activities, both in combatant and non-combatant roles, as members of regular and auxiliary units in the armies of many nations. During World War II tens of thousands of women were enlisted into the Auxiliary Territorial Service, serving with the British Army in a number of trades and categories, which included driving vehicles from light cars to ambulances and lorries. Here are an A.T.S. officer and driver, with a Ford staff car in the background; a prize-winning vignette. The figures are scratch-built from resin castings.

Dilley Collection

Plate 98 – Nick Infield: Napoleonic Soldiers Fishing. 54mm

Proving the point that off-duty scenes can be just as effective as those of violent action, this delightful diorama of soldiers peace-fully fishing has won great acclaim for its youthful creator. The figures are Historex conversions, the water is carefully used clear-resin, and the whole piece has been thoughtfully conceived and executed.

Infield Collection

Plate 99 – R. Jeffries: M4 Sherman Tank 1945. 1/32nd

A well-balanced composition, this diorama features perhaps the best known of all the Allied tanks in a setting representative of almost any urban area of North-west Europe ruined by the cam-paigns of 1944–45. Vehicle, crew and much of the background details are from standard commercial plastic kits, but have been

153

assembled, painted and grouped with skill to result in a most attractive presentation.

A. Campbell Collection

Plate 100 – F. Verlinden: British 6pr Anti-tank Gun in Action 1943. 1/35th

Imaginatively composed from standard plastic-kit items, this is another nicely finished diorama from the hand of François Verlinden. This Belgian modeller's style is unmistakable, and his output – which is very considerable – is sure of a wide measure of acclaim wherever and whenever it appears.

Verlinden Collection

Plate 101 – Ron Skedgel: Indian in the Snow. 77mm

Conveying a powerful impression of wind and cold, Ron Skedgel's composition of a Redskin and his pony in winter is full of character. The Wild West and its inhabitants are fruitful sources of interesting model subjects, and this is a good example.

A. Campbell Collection

Plate 102 – Ron Skedgel: Scout/Hunter. 54mm

Another Western subject, this dioramic presentation is reminiscent of the paintings of Frank McCarthy. Imaginative use of scenic detail to offset the figure work makes this a striking example of its type.

A. Campbell Collection

Plate 103 – Mike Thomas: Officers and Colour, Royal Fusiliers. 54mm

Mike Thomas's work is deservedly becoming very well known internationally among discerning modellers. Specializing in conversion, mostly of plastic basic components, Mike seems to produce a startling amount of work for competitions, and wins a significant number of trophies. This presentation of officers from different periods in the history of a famous British Infantry regiment is typical of Mike's neat and painstaking style.

Thomas Collection

Plate 104 – Brian Owen: W.A.A.C. Dispatch Rider 1918. 54mm

Considered in their time to be rather daring and dashing, if not actually 'fast', the service women of World War I built up a solid tradition of hard work and efficiency that was to stand them in good stead in the years that followed 1918. Brian Owen, a young modeller of ability, has produced several figures of girls in the services of that era, among them this vignette of a dispatch rider pulling on her gauntlets with purposeful air before rushing off on her – for those days – powerful machine.

Owen Collection

Plate 105 – Michael Tadman: 1st Foot Guards, Review Order 1815. 54mm

In stiff drill positions and ornate finery these parading Guardsmen are typical of the élite troops of the Napoleonic period. On campaign, however, they were clothed in a much more business-like fashion, and gave a good account of themselves in some of the hardest fought battles of the Peninsular War and '100 Days'. Mike Tadman's work is extremely clean and 'unfussy', and his choice of subjects is often slanted towards the unusual and amusing.

Tadman Collection

Plate 106 – E. P. Staines: British Women's Land Army Girl 1945. 1/12th

This attractive large-scale figure is representative of the many women's auxiliary units raised during World Wars I and II. Formed to replace the male agricultural workers called to military service, the Women's Land Army helped to keep the farms of Britain in full production. This piece is scratch-built from plastic components, and is one of several figures of service women and auxiliaries produced by E. P. Staines and winning prizes in competitions of the International Plastic Modellers' Society.

Staines Collection

Plate 107 – Cesare Milani: Napoleon's Escape from Waterloo. 54mm

Entitled 'Waterloo–the End', this diorama depicts the scene as the Emperor Napoleon, shielded by the remnants of his Guard, prepares to leave the stricken field. A convincing air of urgency and confusion is conveyed by this example of Cesare's work, which has done well in international competition. The piece is largely made up of converted Historex plastics, with some very neat vehicle building.

Milani Collection

Plate 108 – A. T. Kettle: Elephant Battery in Abyssinia 1860. 54mm

Entirely constructed from converted Britain's plastic figures in a scenic setting, this neat diorama won an important competition of the British Model Soldier Society. Tony Kettle's work, of which other examples are given in these plates, is distinguished by its neatness and ingenuity. The conversion of the elephant from a standing to a kneeling position is a triumph of animation which won warm praise from Ronald Cameron, the designer of the original Britain's model.

Kettle Collection

Plate 109 – Donald Skinner: Panzer IV in the Western Desert. 1/35th

Attractively photographed against a desert background, this is another excellent example of the meticulous modelling work of Donald Skinner. It is an extensively detailed plastic assembly kit and figures, the sign-post adding an evocative touch to the presentation.

Philip O. Stearns Collection

Plate 110 – François Verlinden: Grant Tank 1942. 1/35th
A classic example of what can be made by the careful construction and assembly of standard commercial plastic kits in this imaginatively composed diorama. Accessories and groundwork combine – without overpowering the main subject – to provide a realistic setting for the powerful vehicle.

Verlinden Collection

Plate 111 – D. Davis: 15th Hussars in Undress 1822. 54mm
Basic Historex components, expertly converted and presented, went into the construction of this delightful study. The animation is of a particularly high standard, notably the horse's stance with extended neck, lowered head, and tongue flicking out to explore the trooper's bucket.

Philip O. Stearns Collection

Plate 112 – Eugene Leliepvre: Texel Operations. 54mm
In the early days of 1795, during bitter-cold weather in which the Texel froze over, the French 7th Hussars, in an amazing 'ice-borne' operation, captured the Dutch fleet. The event is brought to life by the combined artistry of Eugene Leliepvre and Rene Gilet, director of Historex.

Historex Collection

Plate 113 – D. Disley: R.H.A. Officer 1807. 75mm
Don Disley is a painstaking painter of figures who delights in presenting his models neatly and cleanly. This Horse Artillery Officer of the Napoleonic period demonstrates how a commercial casting can acquire individuality by the application of a modeller's particular style of finishing.

Disley Collection

Plate 114 – Marcel Baldet: Poilu 1917. 54mm

One of several outstanding French artists producing 'bespoke' figures just after World War II and subsequently, Marcel Baldet has been widely respected for his work by the modelling fraternity. In the piece illustrated he captures the dogged endurance of World War I infantrymen, whatever their nationality.

Philip O. Stearns Collection

Plate 115 – K. Engledow: Queen's Own Hussars. 90mm

An attractive study of a hussar and his mount during the Napoleonic period. Since the soldier is wearing his pelisse, which would normally swing loose from his left shoulder, the intention of the piece must be to indicate inclement weather conditions. True hussar regiments were rare in the British Army of that period, so models of them have an added interest.

Engledow Collection

Plate 116 – Eugene Leliepvre: Figure with Accoutrements. 15cm to 1m

A splendid example of a large-scale mounted figure with extra accoutrements, a type of piece carried out with such precision by this master of the art. In these figurines the basic mannikins are carved from wood, then painted and dressed in clothes and equipment fashioned from real cloth, leather and other relevant materials. Consummate artistry and detailed knowledge of the subject are necessary for the creation of these brilliant works.

Leliepvre Collection

Plate 117 – Eugene Leliepvre: French Drummers. 15cm to 1m

Two more exquisite examples of the master's dressed figurines, these infantry drummers of the eighteenth and early nineteenth centuries have been created with scrupulous attention to stance and uniform detail.

Philip O. Stearns Collection

Plate 118 – Josianne Desfontaines: Venetian Street Scene. 54mm

The work of a highly esteemed 'bespoke' figure creator, these delightful miniatures are also dressed in separate garments, but in the case of Mlle Desfontaines the materials are metal, sheet lead, wire, and so on. That so much delicate and intricate detail can be incorporated into such 'standard' scale pieces is in itself remarkable, and the artist's flair makes each figure a masterpiece in its own right.

Peter Young Collection

Plate 119 – Josianne Desfontaines: War Elephant. 54mm

Representing a subject from the ancient world, this piece is modelled and finished with the care and attention to detail that are characteristic of this artist. Mlle Desfontaines' creations are solid metal castings, animated and painted to result in some of the finest examples of the miniaturist's craft.

Philip O. Stearns Collection

Plate 120 – Josianne Desfontaines: Mediaeval Knights. 54mm

Demonstrating the universality of her talents, these figures (from yet another historical period) by Mlle Desfontaines are excellent reconstructions of fighting men of the mediaeval era.

Philip O. Stearns Collection

Plate 121 – Ray Lamb: Chasseur of the Guard. 54mm

Probably one of the best known of all military miniatures, this magnificent figure, based on Historex plastic components, is modelled after a painting by the famous French artist Gericault. When the piece first appeared it was recognized as quite outstanding by the modelling fraternity, and established a reputation for Ray Lamb, its creator, that has been reinforced with each subsequent item he has produced. A photograph of the model has been used on

159

the cover of the Historex agents' catalogue and made its details familiar all over the modelling world, providing at once an inspiration and a challenge to the miniaturist seeking to acquire the highest standards in his work.

Sangster Collection

Plate 122 – Ray Lamb: Napoleonic Carabiniers. 54mm

This small group shows the consistent excellence of Ray Lamb's attention to details of anatomy, dress and equipment, with particular emphasis on the rendering of textures – techniques much admired by modellers, who practise to master them in their own presentations.

Sangster Collection

Plate 123 – Sheperd Paine: Elite Gendarmes. 54mm

So versatile in his talent is this American modeller – a Grand Master in the competition classifications of the United States – and so prolific his output that it is not easy to select typical examples of his work! In this plate, however, we can see and appreciate Shep Paine's supreme ability to convey the mood and atmosphere of a situation by the positioning and reaction of his figure subjects one with another. One can all but hear what the mounted gendarme is shouting to his sword-drawing colleague! It goes almost without saying that Shep's modelling techniques, painting and presentation, whatever his subject, are impeccable, and the whole military miniature hobby benefits from his instructive leaflets and practical examples.

Sangster Collection

Plate 124 – Sheperd Paine: Trooper Royal Scots Greys 1815. 54mm

An early specimen of Sheperd Paine's work, this piece, constructed from basic Historex plastic components, reveals clearly the sharpness of detail and realism in pose that characterize his figures. These

160

qualities are evident however numerous the pieces or complex the situation that he is depicting.

Sangster Collection

Plate 125 – Pierre Conrad: Lady Godiva. 54mm

Based on Historex components beautifully converted, painted and presented, this scene of Lady Godiva returning to the convent after her historic ride through the streets of Coventry is the work of Pierre Conrad. This artist, a French ex-cavalryman and horse-master of renown whose service includes twenty-seven years in the mounted branch of the *Garde Republicaine*, specializes in figures, groups and dioramas involving horses. He depicts these animals in every conceivable position and phase of motion, bringing to his models all the knowledge and understanding that he has acquired over so many years' association with the real creatures.

Philip O. Stearns Collection

Plate 126 – Pierre Conrad: Trooper, Napoleonic Horse Grenadiers. 54mm

Conrad's feeling for the cavalry service is epitomized by this Napoleonic soldier on his sturdy mount. Utilizing components of Historex and S.E.G.O.M. manufacture in his work, Conrad blends adaptation, animation, and painting to produce unique works of art.

Philip O. Stearns Collection

Plate 127 – Pierre Conrad: Murat and Aide. 54mm

These basic Historex figures, assembled, painted and displayed on a scenic base, are further proof – if such were needed – of Conrad's abilities with equestrian models. The flamboyant Murat with his penchant for exotic, even bizarre, costume is a favourite subject for modellers interested in the Napoleonic era, and this piece of Conrad's does him justice.

Philip O. Stearns Collection

Plate 128 – Charles Stadden: The Death of Nelson 1805. 54mm

Based upon a painting of renown, this composition depicts the cockpit of Nelson's flag-ship 'Victory' at the moment of the hero's death during the Battle of Trafalgar. The figures – metal castings animated and detailed – and the lighting have been grouped and arranged in an effective rendering of this moving episode from naval history.

Courtesy of Stadden

Plate 129 – Eugene Leliepvre: Review by the Emperor. 54mm

This representation of Napoleon 1st reviewing his troops is in effect a carousel, in addition to being a masterly piece of modelling. The troops under review are mounted on a turn-table which, when set in motion, parades them in rotation through the arch, past the figures of the Emperor and his staff, and so on, around and around.

Historex Collection

Plate 130 – Philip O. Stearns: Roman Slave Market. 54mm

One aspect only of an ambitious cased diorama containing no less than sixty-five figures to the same scale but issued by a number of manufacturers, this plate shows in detail the slave marketing platform, around which are clustered guards, sales staff and prospective customers, all set against an attractive scenic back drop. The modeller's skill in composition and rendering in paint of the various textures of flesh, drapery and armour was fully extended in this strikingly vivacious scene, which is now part of the Forbes Tangier Collection.

Forbes Tangier Collection

Plate 131 – Norman Abbey: Press-gang! 54mm

The figures in this cased diorama are all from a series designed by Cliff Sanderson, and have been skilfully painted and grouped in an inn setting by the artist Norman Abbey. Use has been made of perspective to give depth to the room, and the open door reveals an officer commanding the press–gang, posed ironically against a poster calling for volunteer recruits. Facial expressions – running the whole gamut of emotion from fear to, in the case of the officer, downright boredom – have been captured exactly in castings and painting. A forceful interpretation of a scene that must have occurred with great frequency in a period when warships' captains were desperately short of hands to man their vessels.

Courtesy of Military Modelling

Plate 132 – Norman Abbey: Seventeenth Century Tavern. 54mm

Also typical of the combination of Sanderson-designed figures with the artistic abilities of Norman Abbey is this superbly observed and lively scene set in an English inn in the middle of the seventeenth century. Serving wenches hurry about their tasks, and a full house of guests are busily partaking of refreshment of all kinds, some, clearly, can be seen to have over-indulged! Use has been made of fibre-optics to light the chandeliers and candelabra with great effect.

Courtesy of Military Modelling

Plate 133 – Ray Anderson: John of Gaunt. 54mm

The work of an eminent creator of 'bespoke' dioramas, Ray Anderson's scene depicting the consecration to knighthood of a figure in English history, is a classic example of the use of light and positioning to emphasize a subject and create an atmosphere appropriate to the situation. Ray's work is well known and much respected among the modelling fraternity, particularly in his native United States. A superlative craftsman, Ray never produces a piece that is less than outstanding.

Courtesy of Ray Anderson

163

Plate 134 – François Verlinden: M113 Armoured Personnel Carrier. 1/35th

A subject from the war in Vietnam, this model of an American armoured personnel carrier is finished to Verlinden's usual exacting standards. This piece demonstrates yet again the facility possessed by this first-class modeller for creating realistic scenes and interesting situations.

Verlinden Collection

Plate 135 – Philip O. Stearns: Victorian Military Wedding. 54mm

The happy couple moving to their carriage attended by guests and domestic staff, with the occasional passers-by to witness their departure, form the main subject of this interesting diorama, composed of metal figures from several manufacturers. As darkness is falling, the street lamps and lights of the house in the background lend emphasis to the scene and also afford glimpses of room interiors and occupants in a most ingenious presentation. The diorama has been presented by its creator to the National Collection of the British Model Soldier Society and is on view to the public at Hatfield House, one of the great 'stately homes' of England, seat of the Earls of Salisbury.

B.M.S.S./Philip O. Stearns

Plate 136 – Philip O. Stearns: Detail from Roman Slave Market. 54mm

Detail from the diorama also shown in Plate 130, this photograph highlights a military group, with soldiers displaying a sturdy captive to a senior officer as a citizen of Rome observes the scene with interest.

Forbes Tangier Collection

Plate 137 – Roy Dilley: Screw-gun in Action. 54mm

As a finale to this collection of colour pictures we have a short selection of battle scenes. In this plate we see a light mountain-gun of the type made famous by Rudyard Kipling in his poem 'Screw-guns'. The piece and its detachment are depicted as they appeared in the Sudan campaign of 1884–85, when a British expedition set out to the relief of General Gordon at Khartoum. Against the background of the Bayuda desert the gunners get in some practice against distant groups of the enemy, directed by their section officer from his vantage point on a convenient rock. The figures are conversions of plastic Almark Japanese, with metal Rose Model heads, and the gun is an H-R Products item, although the similar-scale weapon by Hinchliffe could have been employed to equal effect.

Dilley Collection

Plate 138 – Edward Suren: Majuba Hill 1881. 30mm

By using smaller figures a better impression of numbers and actual areas covered in a battle can often be achieved more satisfactorily and handily. It is, however, essential that the figures used are accurate in anatomical proportions, and equipment detail. Marketed under the trade-mark Willie Figures, Ted Suren's miniatures exactly fulfil these requirements and are in great demand not only from diorama builders but as collector items in their own right. Depicted is an episode – disastrous to the British – from the conflict with the Boers in South Africa in 1881.

Courtesy of E. Suren

Plate 139 – Edward Suren: The Royal Scots Greys at Waterloo. 30mm

Sweeping in over the trampled corn the Greys charge against the French infantry of the 45th Regiment, an occasion at which Sergeant Ewart captured an 'Eagle', and which is commemorated to this day by an eagle badge worn by the Royal Scots Dragoon Guards, successors to the old 'Greys'.

Courtesy of E. Suren

Plate 140 – Edward Suren: 16th Lancers at Aliwal. 30mm
On 28 January 1846, during the wars against the powerful Sikh forces in North-west India, the British 16th Lancers made a daring and successful charge at the battle of Aliwal. Suren's stirring diorama, cleverly photographed to give an impression of swirling movement and dust-clouds, shows the moment of impact, and is full of exciting detail, action and atmosphere.

Courtesy of E. Suren

Recommended Reading

i. Useful Reference Books

AUTHOR	TITLE AND PUBLISHER
Achilles, Walter	*Zinnfiguren als kulturhistorische Quelle* (Brunswick, 1968).
Alberini, Massimo	*Model Soldiers* (London: Orbis Books, 1972).
Armont, Paul	*Soldats d'hier et d'aujourd'hui* (Paris, 1929).
Baldet, Marcel	*Figurines et Soldats de Plomb* (Paris, 1961).
Bard, Bob	*Making and Collecting Military Miniatures* (New York, 1957).
Blum, Peter	*Military Models* (New York: Odessy Press, 1964).
Carman, William Y.	*British Military Uniforms* (London: Spring Books, 1968).
Carman, William Y.	*Model Soldiers* (London: Charles Letts, 1973).
Cassin-Scott, Jack	*Making Model Soldiers* (London: Stephen Hope, 1973).
Dilley, Roy	*Beginners' Guide to Military Modelling* (London: Pelham, 1974).
Dilley, Roy	*Scale Model Soldiers* (London: Almark, 1972).

Edwards, T. J.   *Standards, Guidons and Colours* (Aldershot: Gale & Polden, 1953).

Ellis, Chris   *How to go Plastic Modelling* (London: Patrick Stephens, 1968).

Ellis, Chris   *How to go Advanced Plastic Modelling* (London: Patrick Stephens, 1970).

Ellis, Chris (ed)   *Model Soldier Manual* (King's Langley: Argus, 1976).

Featherstone, Donald   *Handbook for Model Soldier Collectors* (London: Kaye & Ward, 1969).

Fritzsch, Karl and Manfred Bachmann   *An Illustrated History of Toys* (London, 1965).

Fosten & Dilley   *Dioramas and Scenic Settings* (London: Almark, 1977).

Fosten & Dilley   *Painting and Detailing Military Miniatures* (London: Almark, 1977).

Funcken, L. & R.   *L'Uniforme et les Armes* (series) (Touraine: Casterman, 1968–78).

Garratt, John   *Model Soldiers* (London: Seeley Service, 1959).

Garratt, John   *Model Soldiers for the Connoisseur* (London: Seeley Service, 1972).

Hampe, Theodor   *Der Zinnsoldat* (Berlin: ein Deutsches Sielzug, 1924).

Harris, Henry   *How to go Collecting Model Soldiers* (London: Patrick Stephens, 1969).

Harris, Henry   *Model Soldiers* (London: Weidenfeld & Nicolson, 1962).

Hintze, Erwin   *Die Deutschen Zinngiesser und ihre Marken* (Leipzig, 1921).

Holme, C. Geoffrey   *Children's Toys of Yesteryear* (London & New York, 1932).

Jackson, N.   *Toys of Other Days* (London, 1908).

Jones, Kenneth	*Scale Model Fighting Vehicles* (London: Almark, 1972).
Martin, Paul et M. Vaillant	*Le Monde merveilleux des soldats de plomb* (Paris, 1959).
Muybridge, Eadweard	*Animals in Motion* (Dover & New York, 1957).
Muybridge, Eadweard	*The Human Figure in Motion* (Dover & New York, 1955).
Ortman, Erwin	*Collector's Guide to Model Tin Figures* (Leipzig, 1974).
Quarrie, Bruce (ed)	*Modelling Miniature Figures* (Cambridge: Patrick Stephens, 1975).
Rattelmüller, Paul E.	*Zinnfiguren Die Welt in der Spanschatel* (Munich, 1971).
Richards, Leonard	*Old British Model Soldiers* (London: Arms & Armour, 1970).
Schirmer, Friedrich	*Umgang mit Zinnfiguren* (Burgdorf-Hann, 1967).
Stearns, Philip O.	*How to make Model Soldiers* (London: Hamlyn, 1974).
Tylden, Maj. G.	*Horses and Saddlery* (London: Allen, 1965).
Wells, H. G.	*Little Wars* (London, 1913).
White, Gwen	*A Book of Toys* (London, 1946).
Windrow, Martin and Gerry Embleton	*Model Soldiers* (Cambridge: Patrick Stephens, 1976).

Almark, Blandford and Osprey publish series of books on military subjects, and which can be recommended, and there are, of course, multitudes of books dealing with the various aspects of military life; many of them containing drawings, photographs, prints and textual descriptions that would be of value to modellers. It really is a question of the enthusiast getting to know all he can about his particular interest by means of library services, booksellers' lists, modelling societies, and so on. The great national museums in most countries also operate information services for the serious student. (A stamped and addressed envelope should always accompany any such written query.)

ii Magazines and Periodicals

TITLE	PUBLISHER/TOWN
Airfix Magazine	Unwin, Woking, England.
Campaigns	Marengo Publications, Los Angeles, California, U.S.A.
Gazette des Uniformes	S.E.R.A., Paris, France.
Military Journal	Bennington, Vermont, U.S.A.
Military Modeller	Challenge Publications, Canoga Park, California, U.S.A.
Military Modelling	M.A.P. Ltd, Hemel Hempstead, Herts, England.
Modell-Fan	Bremen, West Germany.
Model Soldier	Ilford, Essex, England.
Model World (o/p)	Almark, London, England.
Replica in Scale	San Antonio, Texas, U.S.A.
Scale Modeller	Challenge Publications, Canoga Park, California, U.S.A.
Scale Models	M.A.P. Ltd, Hemel Hempstead, Herts, England.
Soldier Magazine	H.M.S.O., London, England.
Soldier	Challenge Publications, Canoga Park, California, U.S.A.
Squadron Magazine	Squadron/Signal Publications, Warren, Michigan, U.S.A.
Warrior	Genova, Italy.

Modelling Societies and their Journals

Some enthusiasts like to band together in clubs and societies, a number of which hold regular displays, competitions and other meetings, publish their own journals and, by promoting the free exchange of information and ideas, further the cause of the hobby in many parts of the world. The selection that is listed here, though not by any means comprehensive, gives some indication to the interested reader of where kindred spirits may be found. The name of a society's journal is given where known.

Argentina
Association de Collectionistas y Miniaturistas de la Argentina, Olivos, Buenos Aires, Argentina.

Australia
Military Historical Society of Australia, B. J. Videon, 20 Thomasina Street, Bentley East, Victoria 3165, N.S.W., Australia.

Austria
Austrian Model Soldier Society, Dr. Erich Kroner, 24 Hernalserhauptstrasse, Wien XVII, Austria.
Journal: *1683*.

Belgium

Aide-Memoire du Collectionneur, Brussels, Belgium.

Journal: *Aide-Memoire du Collectionneur.*

Société Belge des Collectionneurs de Figurines, M. Stevelinck, 365 Ave. du Kouter, Brussels, Belgium.

Journal: *La Figurine.*

Canada

Canadian Historical Miniature Figures Society, Vancouver, Canada.

Journal: *Standard.*

Ontario Model Soldier Society, W. Peters, 1 North Glen Ave, Islington, Ontario, Canada.

Journal: *Courier.*

Miniature Armoured Fighting Vehicle Collectors Association, G. Bradford, RR No. 2, Preston, Ontario, Canada.

Denmark

Danish Model Soldier and Uniform Society, Paul lb Leibe, Broderskabsveg 15, Copenhagen F, Denmark.

Journal: *Chakoten.*

Eire (Ireland)

Irish Model Soldier Society, 61 Brighton Road, Rathgar, Dublin.

France

Amicale des Collectionneurs de Figurines du Centre-Loire, Orleans, France.

Journal: *Le Briquet.*

Société des Collectionneurs des Figurines Historiques, M. Philippott, 38 Rue de Lubeck, Paris 16e, France.

Journal: *Bulletin.*

East Germany

Zentraler Arbeitskreis Kulturgeschichtliche Zinnfiguren der Zen-

tralen Kommission Natur und Heimat des Prasidialrates des Kulturbundes der DDR, Berlin, German Democratic Republic.
Journal: *Arbeitsmaterial*.

West Germany
Deutsche Gesellschaft der Freunde und Sammler Kulturhistorischer Zinnfiguren, Fred. Schirmer, 3167, Burgdorf Hann, Wallgartenstrasse 26, German Federal Republic.
Journal: *Die Zinnfigur*.
Vereinigung Freie Zinnfigurensammler e. v., Allersberg, German Federal Republic.
Journal: *Sammlerbrief*.

Great Britain
British Model Soldier Society, J. T. Ruddle, 22 Priory Gardens, Hampton, Middx, England.
Journal: *The Bulletin*.
Miniature Armoured Fighting Vehicle Assn, G. E. G. Williams, 15 Berwick Ave, Heaton Mersey, Stockport, Cheshire, England.
Journal: *Tankette*.
International Plastic Modellers' Society (MM), 16 Maria Theresa Close, New Malden, Surrey KT3 5EF, England.
Journal: *IPMS Magazine*.
Society of Ancients, T. Bath, 11 King Edward's Ave., Millbrook, Southampton, England.
Journal: *Slingshot*.
Military Historical Society, J. W. F. Gaylor, 7 East Woodside, Leighlands, Bexley, Kent, England.
Journal: *The Bulletin*.
International Society of Military Collectors, Tradition, 5 Shepherd Street, Mayfair, London, W1, England.
Scottish Military Collectors' Society, Mitchell S. Davidson, Findon Croft, Findon, Portlethen, Aberdeen AB1 4RN, Scotland.
Journal: *Dispatch*.

Victorian Military Society, John Crouch, 18 Tudor Court, Teddington, Middx TW11 0AH, England.
Journal: *Soldiers of the Queen*.

Society for the Study of the History, Traditions and Regalia of the Forces of the Crown, Elaine Bateson, 18 Fairfield Way, Tadcaster, York, England.
Journal: *Crown Imperial*.

Society for Army Historical Research, c/o The Library, Old War Office Building, Whitehall, London SW1, England.
Journal: *Journal of the Society for Army Historical Research*.

Italy

Club Modellistico, Piero Banfi, Via Battisti, 12–20035 Lissone (M), Italy.

Model Club 7 Nani, Corso Italia, 43 r–17100 Savona, Italy.

Vallebelbo Model Club, Via Nizza, 29–14053 Canelli (Asti), Italy.

Club Modellistico Genova-Est, Via delle Ginestre, 51–16137 Genova, Italy.

Club Modellistico Genovese, Via Gramsci, 29–16126 Genova, Italy.

C.S.I. Model, Via Parma, 32–15100 Alessandria, Italy.

Centre International d'Uniformologie, Torre dei Conti, Largo C. Ricci 44, 00184 Rome, Italy.

Unione Nationale Collezionisti d'Italia, Rome, Italy.
Journal: *La Voce del Collezionista*.

Netherlands

Stichting ter bevordering van de toepassing van kultuur-historische tinnen Figuren, Amstelveen, Netherlands.
Journal: *De Tinnen Tafelronde*.

Spain

Agrupacion de Miniaturistas Militares (Avda), Jose Antonio, 595 (Cupula del Ciliseum), Barcelona, Spain.
Journal: *Boletin*.

Sweden
Drabanten, Nykoping, Sweden.
Journal: *Drabanten.*

Switzerland
Figurina Helvetica, Zurich, Switzerland.
Journal: *Figurina Helvetica.*

United States of America
Military Historical Society of U.S.A., Box 639, Times Square Station, New York 36, U.S.A.
Journal: *Adjutant's Call.*

Company of Military Historians, W. Ogden McCagg, 287 Thayer Street, Providence, Rhode Island, 02906, U.S.A.
Journal: *Military Collector and Historian.*

Miniature Figure Collectors of America, Blair C. Stonier, 2555 Haverford Road, Ardmore, Pennsylvania, 19003, U.S.A.
Journal: *The Guidon.*

National Capital Military Collectors, P.O. Box 241, Silver Spring, Maryland, 20907, U.S.A.
Journal: *Vedette.*

Southern California Military Collectors, David E. Kay, 1628 East First Street, Long Beach, California, U.S.A.
Journal: *California Lancer.*

Military Miniature Society of Illinois, A. W. Neckerman, 8116 Niles Avenue, Skokie, Illinois, 60076, U.S.A.
Journal: *The Scabbard.*

Miniatures Militares, Torrence, California, U.S.A.
Journal: *The Bulletin.*

Guild of Miniature Designers and Collectors, San Francisco, California, U.S.A.
Journal: *The Dispatch Case.*

Some Manufacturers of Military Models

This section contains the names and addresses of some manufacturers currently producing figures and other models in both lead and plastic, together with the principal types that they offer. Most can supply lists of their lines on application (with a stamped and addressed envelope). There are others, of course, and enthusiasts will keep up with the steady stream of newcomers to these ranks through modelling magazines, advertisements and trade papers. Some famous names have, alas, disappeared in recent years, although their products can still be seen in museums and private collections.

Name	Address	Model Types
Airfix Products Ltd	Haldane Place, Garratt Lane, London SW18, England.	1/32nd plastic assembly kits of figures and vehicles.
Alcocer, Lucio	Calle Ciegos de San Cucufato, No 1-bojos, Barcelona 3, Spain.	54mm and 45mm metal figures and equipment.
Almirall, Jose	Rosellon 285 bis, Barcelona, Spain.	54mm metal figures.
Alymers Miniploms	Maestro Lope 7, Bujasot, Spain.	20mm metal figures.
Armtec	31 Locke Drive, Enfield, Connecticut, U.S.A.	1/76th and 1/35th plastic accessories.
Australian Military Miniatures	Berrima District Post, Argylle St, Moss Vale, N.S.W., Australia.	54mm metal figures.

Name	Address	Model Types
Bandai Models	Obtainable world-wide.	Plastic assembly kits.
Beck, Franz	35 Kassel, Reginastrasse 7, Germany.	Flats, *Zinnfiguren*.
Black Watch, The	P.O. Box 666, Van Nuys, California 91408, U.S.A.	90mm metal figures and ordnance.
Blenheim Soldiers	Obtainable from Under Two Flags, St Christopher's Place, Wigmore St, London, England.	54mm metal figures.
Bolling, W.	X 1071, Berlin 71, Germany.	Flats, *Zinnfiguren*.
Braune, H.	X 825, Meissen, Germany.	Flats, *Zinnfiguren*.
Bretignier, P.	Le Gravelot, La Chaussée d'Vory, (Eure et Loire), France.	Flats.
Britain's Ltd	Blackhorse Lane, Walthamstow, London E17, England.	54mm metal and plastic figures and equipment.
British Bulldog Figures	72 Vivian Road, Sketty, Swansea, S. Glamorgan, S. Wales.	54mm metal figures.
Cameron Figures	Obtainable from Tradition, Shepherds Market, London, England.	120mm metal figures.
Cameo Personalities	P.O. Box 3035, Glendale, California 91021, U.S.A.	54mm and 80mm metal portrait figures.
Casa Pardo	Buenos Aires, Argentina.	60mm metal figures.
Cavalier Miniatures	105 Jamaica Ave., New York, N.Y. 11207, U.S.A.	54mm metal figures.
Charles, Al, Figures	Obtainable from Greenwood & Ball, 61 Westbury St, Thornaby on Tees, Teesside, England; and others.	54mm and 80mm metal figures.
Chota Sahib	25 St Paul St, Brighton, Sussex, England.	90mm metal figures.
Cockade Miniatures	P.O. Box 702, Brookline, Massachusetts, 02146, U.S.A.	54mm metal figures.
Coronet Miniatures	P.O. Box 83, Postal Station P, Toronto, Ontario, Canada.	54mm metal figures.
Cumitin, A.	Frau van Baarlen, Meander 317, Amstelveen, Netherlands.	Flats, *Zinnfiguren*.

Name	Address	Model Types
DEK Military Models	71 Vaughan Way, Leicester, England.	80mm metal figures.
Dixon Miniatures	Ash Grove, Royles Head Lane, Longwood, Huddersfield, Yorkshire, England.	25mm metal figures.
Dorset Soldiers	Obtainable from Under Two Flags, St Christopher's Place, Wigmore St, London, England.	54mm metal figures.
Dragoon Models	P.O. Box 24, Trylan Close, Ilford, Essex, England.	100mm metal figures.
Droste, Dr med V.	7142 Marbach/Neckar, Grinterstrasse 3, Germany.	Flats, *Zinnfiguren*.
Eagle Miniatures	P.O. Box 14, Barry, S. Glamorgan, Wales.	54mm metal figures.
Elastolin	O & M Hausser, Neustadt/Coburg, Jahreswende, Germany.	40mm and 60mm plastic figures, etc.
Ensign Miniatures	5 Market Place, Woburn, Milton Keynes, England.	54mm metal figures.
Eriksson, Holgar	Sommerovagen 8, Karlstad, Sweden.	30mm, 40mm, 54mm metal figures, etc.
E.S.C.I.	Obtainable worldwide.	1/35th and 1/76th plastic assembly kits.
Fischer, H.	8 Munchen 12, Zschokkerstrasse 40/or, Germany.	Flats, *Zinnfiguren*.
Fohler, Frau Edith	A1130 Wien, Lainzerstrasse 171, Austria.	Flats, *Zinnfiguren*.
Fritz, M. E.	7 Stuttgart 13, Plankstrasse 71, Germany.	Flats, *Zinnfiguren*.
Greenwood & Ball	61 Westbury St, Thornaby on Tees, Teesside, England.	54mm and 80mm metal figures, etc.
Grunewald, R.	3001 Elze-Brennemuhlen b, Hannover NR 231b, Germany.	Flats, *Zinnfiguren*.
Hafer, W.	3500 Kassel-Oberwehre, Felsburgstrasse 15, Germany.	Flats, *Zinnfiguren*.
Hall, Charles	12 Paisley Terrace, Edinburgh, Scotland, G.B.	54mm metal figures.
H. A. M. Miniatures Inc.	76–15 85 Drive, Woodhaven, New York 11421, U.S.A.	54mm metal figures.

178

Name	Address	Model Types
Hearne Originals	Ponchydown House, Blackborough, Nr Cullompton, Devon, England.	90mm, 120mm metal figures.
Heller	Obtainable world-wide.	1/35th plastic assembly kits.
Heritage Models	9840 Monroe Drive, Bldg 106, Dallas, Texas, U.S.A.	25mm metal figures.
Heroics & Ros Figures	P.O. Box 26, Rectory Road, Beckenham, Kent, England.	1/300th metal figures and vehicles.
Hinchliffe Models Ltd	Meltham, Huddersfield, Yorkshire, England.	15mm, 20mm, 54mm, 75mm metal figures, guns, etc.
Hinton Hunt Figures	Rowsley, River Road, Taplow, Bucks, England.	20mm, 54mm metal figures.
Historex	23 Rue Petain, Paris XI, France.	54mm plastic figures, guns, etc.
Historex Agents	3 Castle St, Dover, England.	54mm plastic figures, guns, etc.
H.R. Products Inc	9232 Waukegan Road, Morton Grove, Illinois, 60053, U.S.A.	54mm metal weapons, figures, etc.
Imrie/Risley Miniatures	114–05 101st Ave., Richmond Hill, Queens, New York 11419, U.S.A.	54mm metal figures.
Jane Jackson Miniatures	P.O. Box 94, Niagara Falls, Ontario, Canada.	54mm metal figures.
Kilmore Miniatures	P.O. Box 6, Great Missenden, Bucks, England.	90mm metal figures.
Kolbitz, Karlheinz	X1058 Berlin, Dunkerstrasse 4, Germany.	Flats, *Zinnfiguren*.
Kramer Figures	Obtainable from H.R. Products Inc., 9232 Waukegan Road, Morton Grove, Illinois, 60053, U.S.A.	54mm metal figures.
Lamming Miniatures	254 Wincolmlee, Hull, England.	20mm, 25mm metal figures.
Lasset Miniatures	Obtainable from Greenwood & Ball, 61 Westbury St, Thornaby on Tees, Teesside, England; and others.	54mm metal figures.
Maier, Sixtus & Tilo	851 Furth (Bayern), Postfach 35, Germany.	Flats, *Zinnfiguren*.

179

Name	Address	Model Types
Mark Time Figures	147 The Glade, Shirley, Croydon, Surrey, England.	54mm metal figures, accessories, etc.
Mignot, Maison	1 Rue de Vieux Columbia, Paris 6me, France.	54mm metal figures.
Miniature Americana	P.O. Box 2061, Mount Prospect, Illinois 60056, U.S.A.	54mm metal figures.
Miniature Figurines	1–5 Graham Road, Southampton, England.	25mm metal figures, equipment, etc.
Minot Miniatures	P.O. Box 25, Watling St, Boreham Wood, Herts, England.	25m, 54mm metal figures, etc.
M. J. Mode Figures	198 Kimberley Road, Leicester, England.	54mm metal figures.
M & M Models	27 Gilbert Ave., Tuxford, Nr Newark, Notts, England.	25mm metal figures.
Model Figures & Hobbies	Lower Balloo Road, Groomsport, Co. Down, N. Ireland.	25mm, 54mm metal figures and equipment.
Minimen	P.O. Box 451, Chagrin Falls, Ohio 44022, U.S.A.	100mm metal figures.
Monarch Miniatures	P.O. Box 4195, Long Island City, New York 11104, U.S.A.	54mm, 80mm metal figures.
Monogram Corporation	Morton Grove, Illinois, U.S.A.	54mm metal and plastic figures and kits.
Neckel, Friedrich	7321 Hattenhofen, Wandlingen, Germany.	Flats, *Zinnfiguren*.
New Hope Design	Rothbury, Northumberland, England.	54mm metal figures.
Nostalgia Figures	37 Davis Road, Acton, London W3, England.	54mm metal figures.
Ochel, A.	23 Kiel, Feldstrasse 24b, Germany.	Flats, *Zinnfiguren*.
Phoenix Model Developments	The Square, Earls Barton, Northampton, England.	25mm, 30mm, 54mm, 80mm metal figures.
Piper, John Ltd	2 Acre Road, Kingston-on-Thames, England.	1/100th, 54mm metal vehicles and accessories.
Poste Militaire	Farm View, Station Road, Northiam, Nr Rye, E. Sussex, England.	90mm metal figures.

Name	Address	Model Types
Powell, Bob	11 Daff Ave., Moorabin, Victoria, Australia.	54mm metal figures.
Quality Model Soldiers	439 Shetcliffe Lane, Brierley, Bradford, Yorks, England.	54mm metal figures.
Ral Partha	3642 Hyde Park Ave., Cincinnati, Ohio 45208, U.S.A.	15mm, 25mm metal figures.
Realmodels	32 Thurloe Place, London SW7, England.	54mm, 80mm, 90mm metal figures.
Revell/Italieri	Obtainable world-wide.	1/35th plastic figure and vehicle kits.
Rifle Miniatures di Parasini	Via Ciancuillo 39/8, 16133 Genova, Italy.	54mm metal figures.
Rocchiero, G. M.	Via Cairoli 11/4, 16124 Genova, Italy.	54mm metal figures.
Romund, Karl	3 Hannover, Laverstrasse 19, III, Germany.	Flats, *Zinnfiguren*.
Rose Miniatures	15 Llanover Road, Plumstead, London SE18, England.	25mm, 54mm metal figures.
Sanderson, Cliff, Figures	Obtainable from Greenwood & Ball, 61 Westbury St, Thornaby on Tees, Teesside, England.	54, 80mm metal figures.
Scottish Soldiers	10 Midlothian Drive, Shawlands, Glasgow, Scotland.	54mm, 75mm, 90mm metal figures.
Scruby, Jack	Box 89, 2044, S. Linwood Ave., Visalia, California 93277, U.S.A.	20mm, 25mm, 30mm metal figures.
S.E.G.O.M.	50 Boulevard Malesherbe, Paris 8me, France.	54mm plastic assembly kits.
Sentry Box	112 Holland Road, London W14, England.	54mm, 90mm metal figures.
Series 77 Miniatures	7861 Alabama Ave., No 14, Canoga Park, California 91304, U.S.A.	77mm metal figures.
Skytrex Ltd	28 Brook St, Wymeswold, Leicestershire, England.	25mm metal figures, etc.
Soldatini Berruto	C. Regina Margherita 7, 10124 Torino, Italy.	54mm metal figures.
Soldiers, Soldiers	36 Kennington Road, Lambeth, London SE1, England.	54mm metal figures.

Name	Address	Model Types
Squadron/Rubin Miniatures	3461 East Ten Mile Road, Warren, MI 48091, U.S.A.	54mm metal figures.
Stadden, Chas. C.	Hamilton Marriott, 8 Hale Lane, London NW7, England.	80mm metal figures.
Stadden Figures	Obtainable from Tradition, 5 Shepherd Street, London W1, England.	30mm, 54mm, 80mm metal figures.
Steadfast Soldiers	46 Champion Hill, London SE5, England.	54mm metal figures.
St. George Miniatures	Casella Postale 488, Milano, Italy.	54mm metal figures.
Strombecker Corporation	4646 West Lake St, Chicago, Illinois 60641, U.S.A.	54mm plastic figures.
Tamiya Corporation	Obtainable world-wide.	1/35th plastic assembly kits.
Thomas Industries	Box 7, Shawnee, Oklahoma, U.S.A.	21mm metal figures.
Timpo (Model Toys)	Torbthie Road, Shotts, Lanarkshire, Scotland.	54mm plastic figures and equipment.
Tobinnus, G.	3 Hanover, Gretchenstrasse 25, Germany.	Flats, *Zinnfiguren*.
Tomker Accessories	Verbondstraat 68, 2000 Antwerp, Belgium.	75mm, 80mm, 90mm metal accessories.
Tradition Figures	5 Shepherd's Market, Mayfair, London W1, England.	54mm, 90mm metal figures.
Valiant Miniatures	5118 West Irving Park Road, Chicago, Illinois, 60641, U.S.A.	54mm metal figures.
Verlinden (D.C.S.)	Berlaarsestraat 17, 2500 Lier, Belgium.	54mm plastic scenic accessories.
Warrior Miniatures	25 Grove Road, Leighton Buzzard, Bedfordshire, England.	20mm, 25mm metal figures, etc.
Willie Figures	13/34 Sloane Court West, London SW3, England.	30mm metal figures.
W.M.H. Models	177 Boston Road, Hanwell, London W7, England.	90mm metal figures.

Index

(Figures in bold type refer to colour plate numbers and corresponding plate descriptions.)